Hope in God

A Biblical Perspective for Understanding, Overcoming & Preventing Depression

Kristie Gant

Hope in God

A Biblical Perspective for Understanding,
Overcoming & Preventing Depression

Kristie Gant

Hope in God: A Biblical Perspective for Understanding, Overcoming & Preventing Depression

A Teacher/Leader/Discipler Guide for this study is available at:
www.athomestudies.com

To
Stephanie, Amber,
Gail and Patsy

Table of Contents

About this Study

Hope in God presents biblical principles necessary for dealing with the spiritual aspects of depression. It is designed for individual study, one-on-one discipleship or counseling, and Bible study groups of all sizes.

Each lesson contains three interrelated, yet stand-alone sections. The three sections are:

Foundation Study: These studies provide biblical insights into depression and related issues. Each one is divided into three parts, each part requiring approximately 15 minutes of study.

Name of God: Following each foundational lesson is a section directing you to Scripture passages about God and His character, which will help you to trust Him more fully. *"And those who know Your name will put their trust in You; For You, LORD, have not forsaken those who seek You."*—Psalm 9:10

Topic on Hope: The final section in each lesson is a topical study on a subject related to hope. Each topic is designed to strengthen and increase your hope in God.

The sections make this course extremely flexible and adaptable to any circumstance, ability, individual or group. See page ten for various study options.

Materials required for this study are:

A Bible
A *Hope in God* course book
A pencil or pen

Shorter study options are provided in some sections for those with limited study time or ability. When assignments contain both boldface and non-boldface passages, completing only the boldface items will provide a good overview of essential truths. *(See page 86 for an example.)*

Psalm 61 is a psalm of hope which King David wrote at a low point in his life. Each weekly lesson encourages memorization of a portion of this psalm, using simple repetition. By the end of the seven lessons, you should know the passage well. We pray that it will be a source of continuing hope and encouragement to you.

Journal pages for thoughts, meditations and prayers are provided throughout the course book. Use these to record personal thoughts and insights as you study.

Prayer is vital. Begin and end each of your study times with prayer. It is also a good idea to ask one or more people to pray for you regularly as you study.

for Bible Study Groups and Discipling

For groups with at least 90 minutes for class discussion:

Five days of homework

Complete the Foundation Study (Parts One through Three), along with the corresponding Name and Topic. For example, the first week's homework would consist of:

- Foundation—Lesson One
  (pages 15-24, three days of study)
- Name—Lesson One
  (pages 25-28, one day of study)
- Topic—Lesson One
  (pages 29-35, one day of study)

Cover the Foundation Study during the first half of class. After a break, discuss the Name and Topic. *(Note: It is best to have at least 45 minutes per half.)* [1]

The entire course will be complete after seven weeks of study.

For large classes, groups with less than 90 minutes for class discussion, or groups desiring shorter homework assignments:

Take one week to complete the Foundation Study and the next week to complete the corresponding Name and Topic. For example, the first week's homework would consist of:

- Foundation—Lesson One (pages 15-24)

The second week's homework would consist of:

- Name—Lesson One (pages 25-28)
- Topic—Lesson One (pages 29-35)

The entire course will be complete after fourteen weeks of study.

for Counseling

For those with mild to moderate depression:

Five days of homework

Each week, have counselees complete the Foundation Study, along with the corresponding Name and Topic. For example, the first week's homework would consist of:

- Foundation—Lesson One
  (pages 15-24, three days of study)
- Name—Lesson One
  (pages 25-28, one day of study)
- Topic—Lesson One
  (pages 29-35, one day of study)

The entire course will be complete after seven weeks of study. [1]

For those with moderate to severe depression, or for use with supplemental assignments:

Three segments of homework

Each week, have counselees complete only the three-part Foundation Study. After completion of these basic studies, have counselees complete the Names of God and the Topics on Hope (along with weekly counseling or as homework for follow-up visits). Tapes, journaling, or related readings may easily be assigned with this option (helpful when also addressing issues such as anxiety, worry, etc.).

For those struggling with deep depression, or anything that limits ability for study:

Each week have counselees complete Part One of the Foundation Study, along with the question marked with a ⬡ (located either in Part Two or Three).

After completing this abbreviated course of study, have counselees return to the beginning of the book and complete the questions previously omitted.

*O*f course, there are other possible options and combinations. Feel free to adapt the study options to your particular situation and need.

May the Lord bless your study!

Introduction

Depression is an increasing problem with complicated and variable causes.

Many people—young and old, rich and poor, male and female—have battled or are currently battling depression. This is not a new problem: people throughout biblical, church and world history have experienced periods of profound depression.

All people experience some feelings of depression or "down" days from time to time.

Depression may accompany physical ailments or problems such as anemia, gout, hyper/hypoglycemia, hypothyroidism, lupus, Parkinson's disease, poor diet, vitamin deficiency, fatigue and loss of sleep. In addition, certain medications may cause feelings of depression as a side effect.

If you are experiencing ongoing feelings of depression, consult a physician to treat and/or rule out any physical causes.

If you are currently taking medication, adhering to a special diet or exercise regimen, or following other directions as prescribed by your physician, DO NOT STOP OR ALTER ANY PART OF YOUR MEDICAL TREATMENT WITHOUT CONSULTING YOUR PHYSICIAN.

Depression may also be the result of unbiblical habits or sinful responses to circumstances or people. In these cases, one can only overcome depression by dealing biblically with sin and beginning to live according to biblical principles.

Regardless of its cause, depression always has a spiritual dimension. Because of this, responding to depression in a biblical manner is essential. We must view our circumstances in light of God's Word and live in obedience to it (whether we feel like it or not!). Depression is never an excuse to live or act unbiblically. We must always bring glory to God and encourage and build one another up in the Lord.

Some common synonyms which people may use to describe depression are:

disappointment	melancholy	downcast
heaviness	disheartened	overwhelmed
the blues	sorrowful	tired
alone/loneliness	sad	at a breaking point
numb	thoughts of suicide	gloom/darkness
despair	hopeless	fallen countenance
out of it	guilt	emotionally drained
feeling down	life is meaningless	just don't care
trapped	unmotivated	filled with tears
empty	discouraged	isolation

Do any of the above synonyms fit you? If so, put a check mark by any expressions with which you can identify.

How many did you mark?

Though words can describe depression, it is most important to find out how God describes it, what He says about it, and how He says to deal with and overcome it.

As you complete this study,

May your understanding of the Scriptures increase greatly

May you come to trust more fully in God alone for salvation, joy and deliverance

May your hope in God be kindled, renewed, refreshed and/or strengthened
   and

May you come to know God in such a way that your life will never be the same!

Kristie

Hope
in God

Lessons One through Seven

Hear my cry, O God;
Attend to my prayer.

From the end of the earth I will cry to You,
when my heart is overwhelmed;
Lead me to the rock that is higher than I.

For you have been a shelter for me,
A strong tower from the enemy.

I will abide in Your tabernacle forever;
I will trust in the shelter of Your wings.

Psalm 61:1-4

Lesson One

Where Is Your God?

"Find rest, O my soul, in God alone; my hope comes from Him."

Psalm 62:5 NIV

*"C*all Katie." "Call Katie."

The thought kept returning as I busily tried to finish chores around the house so that I could get going on errands that had to be completed before time to pick up the kids.

"You really should call Katie."

I had no time to call. There was not time today to ask her to lunch or even to spend time talking on the phone. Could I call someone I didn't know well and ask her if she just wanted to join me in my normal busyness? That seemed a bit strange, but I finally gave in. I called. I told her I had been thinking about her and asked her if she would like to run errands with me.

To my surprise, she said "yes." Months later, having become close friends, she confided to me that on the day I called, she was planning to commit suicide.

There are times when life is miserable. In our own ways, we all know this first hand. We each could make a list of our own trials and sufferings: some big, some small, some just big to us. For instance, my list would include:

• not only being born to a military father, but marrying a military man. That ultimately meant 23 moves in 42 years...and consequently, few close friends to call my own

• my parent's refusal to let me wear eye make-up when I started eighth grade (Don't laugh! At the time this was tragic!)

- the terrible storm that broke out our front picture windows

- the tearful good-byes as the government sent my dad to war, not once but twice (I saved the tissues I used to dry my tears in a small apricot-colored box. The day he came home, I threw them away as I thanked the Lord for his return.)

- my grandfather's heart attack and death right after we shared a Sunday dinner during my first semester in college

- my first pregnancy ending in a miscarriage while my husband was overseas

- bathing a child in tepid water for hours, praying for her fever to drop below 105 degrees

- having to move my children away from their friends with each new assignment

- my grandmother's battle with Alzheimer's...and my mom's battle with guilt over decisions that had to be made for her

- my son's being diagnosed with Crohn's disease

- my husband's sudden unemployment due to economic downsizing

- the heartache of having unsaved family members

- the shared heartaches of other friends and family members as they went through their own struggles

Your list may be longer or shorter. There are always those who have suffered less—and always those who have suffered more. Sometimes, suffering is a consequence of our own sinful actions or the sinful actions of others. Other times, God sovereignly designs our trials to further His kingdom, conform us to His image and bring glory to Himself and ultimate good to us.

Regardless, no suffering is wasted and no situation is without hope. That's a truth I have learned to live by daily. And today, Katie does, too!*

Almighty God,

As I come to study Your Word today,
open my understanding that I might know the truths I need to live by, and
touch my heart that I might love You more.

*See Appendix A for a message from the real "Katie."

PART ONE

> "Hear _____ _____, O God; attend to my prayer."
> Psalm 61:1

*D*epression is not a new phenomenon. Many people in the Bible were depressed: Job, Elijah, Cain, Hamaan, Hannah, Luke, King Saul, Jeremiah, David, the disciples on the road to Emmaus and many more.

Romans 15:4 and 1 Corinthians 10:11 tell us that things recorded in the Old Testament are examples for us, that we might learn from them and be instructed and encouraged in our lives today.

> *"For whatever things were written before were written for our learning,*
> *__that we__ through the patience and comfort of the Scriptures __might have hope__."*
> Romans 15:4

Begin your study by learning from an Old Testament believer who struggled with depression.[1]

1. Read Psalm 42.
Beside each phrase below, write out the exact words the psalmist uses to describe how he feels:
(verse references are in parentheses, and the first one is done for you)

   a. spiritually dry (42:1-2)   *"so pants my soul" "my soul thirsts"*

   b. constantly tearful (42:3) _____

   c. forsaken by God and others (42:3) _____

   d. in despair (42:4) _____

   e. longing for past joy and closeness to God (42:4) _____

   f. miserable and without peace (42:5) _____

   g. like he's drowning (42:7) _____

2. Have you experienced any of the feelings described by the psalmist? If so:

   a. Put a check mark in the margin beside all that apply.

   b. When you have had these feelings, how have you responded to them?

3. The psalmist expressed great anguish of soul and sorrow of heart. Where was his God? Was there help? In the first half of verse 5 he asks himself,

"Why are you cast down, O my soul? And why are you disquieted within me?"

How does he answer himself in the last half of this verse?

4. In Part Two's study, you will take a more detailed look at the psalmist's responses. For now, however, end your time with a short prayer. Thank God that, through His Word, you can know that godly people have struggled with depression. Thank Him for including the writings of Old Testament believers for your instruction and encouragement today. When you finish praying, initial the box.

```
┌──────────┐
│          │
│          │
└──────────┘
```


PART TWO

```
┌──────────────────────────────────────────────────────────────────────┐
│                                                                        │
│  " _____ my cry , O God; attend to _____  _____."│
│                          Psalm 61:1                                    │
│                                                                        │
└──────────────────────────────────────────────────────────────────────┘
```

*T*oday you will see how the psalmist responded to his feelings of depression. There is much to learn here, so don't give up!

1. Return to Psalm 42 and record the psalmist's responses below.

Response #1... Psalm 42:5a *(NOTE: The "a" indicates the first half of the verse. A "b" means the last half.)*
He reasons with himself, searching out the cause of his depression. Write down the questions that he asks himself.

Response #2... Psalm 42:5b
He expresses hope in God along with hope that his present troubles will not last forever. Again, write out his exact words below.

18

Response #3... Psalm 42:6

He remembers God's past faithfulness to him and other believers. Read verse 6 out loud.
Write out the phrase about remembering God.

Response #4... Psalm 42:8

He expresses confidence in God.
a. What is he confident God will do for him in the daytime?

b. Does he expect that God will leave him alone at night? What does he say?

Response #5... Psalm 42:8b-9

He prays.
a. What two names for God does he use?

b. Would you describe this prayer as one of praise, request, or questioning?

Response #6... Psalm 42:11a

He examines and reasons with himself again.   This time, write out his two questions using
your own words.

Response #7... Psalm 42:11b

He encourages himself by telling himself what he needs to hear: truth about God, God's
character and the future. Record the truths he tells himself using your own words.

2. Compare your own responses to feelings of depression to the responses of the psalmist. For each response, put an **X** under the appropriate column.

The Psalmist   *How often is this my response?*

	Never	Sometimes	Often	Always
Examines and reasons with himself				
Expresses hope in God				
Expects a better future				
Remembers God's past faithfulness				
Expresses faith and confidence in God				
Prays using the names of God				
Repeatedly tells himself truth				

3. From what you have read:

   a. Would you say the psalmist had given up hope? Why or why not?

   b. Would you say he was taking an active or passive role in overcoming his depression? Support your answer from Scripture.

   c. Do you think God wants you to take an active or passive role in overcoming feelings of depression? Why?

4. Again, close your study time in prayer. Begin with this week's memory verse, and end by telling God that you desire to respond to any feelings of depression in ways that will bring honor to Him. When you finish praying, initial the box.

PART THREE

> *"Hear my _____ , O _____ ; _____ to my prayer."*
>
> Psalm 61:1

*H*ave you ever hoped that life would change or get better?

Have you prayed, asking God to make it so? And then, if it perhaps did not get better, or it improved only temporarily, has your hope been shipwrecked, dashed against a rock?

Has your hope been dashed so many times, or so profoundly, that you have no more hope?

If so, then you are not hoping in God...you are hoping in changed circumstances. True hope is in God, whether or not the circumstances change.

But how does someone find hope in God when it seems that hope is lost?

1. Circle the two phrases which identify the source of the psalmist's strength and hope.

> *"My soul melts from heaviness;*
> *Strengthen me according to Your word...*
>
> *My soul faints for Your salvation,*
> *But I hope in Your word."*
>
> Psalm 119:28, 81

2. How does God's Word bring hope? For one thing, it informs the heart and mind of truths about God.

a. As you read the following passage, circle each truth about God.

> *"Have you not known? Have you not heard?*
> *The everlasting God, the LORD,*
> *The Creator of the ends of the earth,*
> *Neither faints nor is weary.*
> *His understanding is unsearchable. He gives power to the weak,*
> *And to those who have no might He increases strength."*
>
> Isaiah 40:28-29

b. How many truths did you circle?

c. Although *all* of these are truths believers need to keep in mind every day, put a star by the truth that brings the most hope or is the most meaningful to your life at this moment.

d. Why did you pick that truth to star?

3. Teach yourself to respond in a biblical way to your feelings of depression. Reason with yourself. Tell yourself the truths from God's Word that you have just read...truths that will, little by little, bring hope. Help yourself to hear the truths of Scripture by saying the following to yourself (out loud):

God is the everlasting God, Creator of all things.

God is always able to help those who call on Him because He never faints nor gets weary.

God understands and knows all things.

God gives power to the weak.

God increases the strength of those with no might.

Repeat truths such as these to yourself time and time again throughout your day. If possible, say them out loud each time. It doesn't matter whether you feel that these words are true. What matters is that they are true, and your heart needs to hear them.

4. All of the promises in God's Word are sure and certain, but we must remember that God has a timetable for the fulfillment of His purposes. He knows the purposes that are to be accomplished through the circumstances He causes or allows. He has a way and a time for everything.

"But when the time of the promise drew near which God had sworn to Abraham..."

"But when the fullness of the time had come, God sent forth His Son..."

"Behold, the days are coming...that I will perform that good thing which I have promised..."

Acts 7:17, Galatians 4:4, Jeremiah 33:14

In the next lesson, you will look more at the subject of waiting patiently for God's work to be accomplished. For now, however, take a short look at how a believer named Asaph responded when he began to doubt while waiting for God to fulfill His promises. Read Psalm 77:7-15 and list the things the psalmist told himself when his doubts began. *(Your list will come from verses 11-15.)*

Asaph's Example: Truths to Remember When Doubt Begins

5. Whether in times of doubt or strong faith, one of the best uses you can make of your memory is to bring to mind truths about the LORD. Think back and recall at least one act of faithfulness you have seen God work in your life. Record it below.

6. To simply read, remember or repeat Scripture is not all that we need when hope is weak. Many people have read the words on the pages of the Bible and not come away with hope. Why? Because hope is ultimately a gracious gift of God within the heart.

Every believer receives the gift of hope through Jesus Christ at salvation.

> *"Now may our Lord Jesus Christ Himself, and our God and Father, who has loved us and **given** us...good hope by grace, comfort your hearts..."*
>
> 2 Thessalonians 2:16-17a

The gospel message *is* a message of hope! (1 Peter 1:3, Colossians 1:5) In addition, there are several things that will help that gift of hope grow, strengthen and flourish. The main one is to be in God's Word, for it is there that we learn truths about God on which to rely as we wait for Him to act.

What are some of the truths that believers must remember about God in order to consistently place their hope in Him? Record what you learn from the following verses.

Passage   *Truths About God*

a. Deuteronomy 32:3b-4

> *"...Ascribe greatness to our God. He is the Rock,*
> *His work is perfect; For all His ways are justice,*
> *A God of truth and without injustice;*
> *Righteous and upright is He."*

b. Jeremiah 29:11 NIV

> *"'For I know the plans I have for you,' declares the*
> *LORD, 'plans to prosper you and not to harm you,*
> *plans to give you hope and a future.'"*

c. Hebrews 10:23

> *"Let us hold fast the confession of our hope*
> *without wavering, for He who promised is faithful."*

d. Isaiah 55:8-9

> *"'For My thoughts are not your thoughts,*
> *Nor are your ways My ways,' says the LORD.*
> *'For as the heavens are higher than the earth,*
> *So are My ways higher than your ways,*
> *And My thoughts than your thoughts.'"*

7. Would you pray the following prayer as you close your study? Be sure to initial the box when you are done.

O God, My God,

> *Cause me to hope in Your Word and cling to Your promises. You are my hope—may my heart come to know it! Help me to remember Your power, mercy, mighty acts and faithfulness to all generations. As I study Your Word, increase my hope!*

Thoughts, Meditations and Prayers

The LORD of Hosts The God of Jacob

*P*salm 46 reveals a wonderful two-fold name of God: The LORD of hosts, The God of Jacob.

Read the beginning of this psalm out loud:

> *"God is our refuge and strength,*
> *A very present help in trouble.*
> *Therefore we will not fear,*
> *Even though the earth be removed,*
> *And though the mountains be carried into the midst of the sea;*
> *Though its waters roar and be troubled,*
> *Though the mountains shake with its swelling."*

Now read the last verse:

> *"The LORD of hosts is with us;*
> *The God of Jacob is our refuge."*

The "LORD of hosts, the God of Jacob" is the God who is with us and gives refuge when the "earth be removed" and the "waters roar." In other words, He is with us in the midst of turmoil and overwhelming circumstances. He is with us when our lives seem hopeless and even terrifying. Who is He?

1. First, consider the name "LORD." This is the covenant name of God that the Jewish people most revere. As God's covenant name, it reveals God's relationship with His people and His faithfulness to His promises.

It is a word written YHWH, when copying letter-for-letter from the Hebrew. The end result is the name Yahweh (or Jehovah in English). English Bibles usually translate it "LORD" (in all capitals).

Its root is not a noun, like most names, but a verb, carrying the idea of a God who is, always has been and always will be. It is the name God used with Moses at the burning bush when He said, I AM WHO I AM." (Exodus 3:14)

Underline one fact about the name "LORD" that you find most interesting.

2. The word translated "hosts" is "sabaoth." (Therefore, the whole name "LORD of hosts" is Jehovah-Sabaoth.) Who or what are the hosts that God is LORD of? The answer has several parts.

a. In Deuteronomy 4:19, "host" refers to things in the heavens. As you read this verse, circle the things specifically mentioned that are a part of the host of heaven.

> *"And take heed, lest you lift your eyes to heaven, and when you see the sun,*
> *the moon, and the stars, all the host of heaven, you feel driven to worship them..."*

b. In Luke 2:10-15, "host" refers to angels.   Read this well-known passage along with Psalm 103:19-22. Note what the angels are doing in each passage, along with any other insights.

c. "Host" is also used in reference to armies and/or the people of God. Depending on the translation, this word is translated "armies," "camp" or "people." (***NOTE:*** Two examples where the word "host" is used this way and is also translated "host" are Exodus 7:4 NAS and Joshua 3:2 KJV. You may read these up if time permits.)

3. So, Jehovah-Sabaoth (The LORD of hosts) is the LORD of the heavens, the LORD of angels, and the LORD of men. In Psalm 46, the NIV translates the name "LORD of hosts" as "the LORD Almighty." Knowing what you do about the meaning of "hosts," why do you think the translators might have chosen to translate it this way?

4. In Psalm 46, the name that accompanies "LORD of hosts" is "God of Jacob." Briefly record what you know about Jacob (even if you only know his name and that he has a God!). Then, record additional facts from the verses that follow: (For those with limited time, you may complete only Scripture passages in boldface print.)

Facts about Jacob

a. What I know about Jacob

b. Genesis 25:24-27

c. **Genesis 27:35-36**

d. **Genesis 29:30-34**

5. The Almighty L ORD of hosts was the God of this man Jacob. The L ORD of heaven, angels and men took interest in and cared for a simple, solitary man, a man who lived in tents, who was deceitful, and who acted uncaringly toward his wife.

Jacob was a man like any other man, and yet the L ORD of hosts openly identifies Himself as *Jacob's* God.

From the following verses, identify and record some of the actions that are associated with God when He uses the name "the God of Jacob."

a. Psalm 20:1-2a

"May the L ORD answer you in the day of trouble;
May the name of the God of Jacob defend you;
May He send you help from the sanctuary..."

b. Psalm 46:11

"The L ORD of hosts is with us;
The God of Jacob is our refuge."

c. Psalm 84:8

"O L ORD God of hosts, hear my prayer;
Give ear, O God of Jacob!"

d. Psalm 146:5

"Happy is he who has the God of Jacob for his help,
Whose hope is in the L ORD his God,"

6. Here is the most exciting truth for every believer: The God of Jacob is *your* refuge, too. He is your God. The same God that created and upholds the sun/moon/stars, commands legions of angels and rules the world of men is the God who cares about you when life is overwhelming!

The writer of Psalm 42 said, "...they say to me all day long, 'Where is your God?'" Perhaps you have even asked yourself this question.

If someone saw you going through a tough time and said to you, "Where is your God?" how would you now answer? Would you say that God is with you just as He was with Jacob? That He is the Almighty L ORD of hosts who is also the God of individual people, including you?

From the following verses, record other truths you could tell yourself or someone else who asks, "Where is your God?"

Where is your God?

a. Deuteronomy 31:6

"Be strong and of good courage,
do not fear nor be afraid of them;
for the L ORD your God,
He is the One who goes with you.
He will not leave you nor forsake you."

b. Psalm 46:1

"God is our refuge and strength,
A very present help in trouble."

c. Psalm 121 (only a portion is printed below)

> *"...He who keeps you will not slumber...*
> *The LORD is your keeper;*
> *The LORD is your shade at your right hand..."*

d. Psalm 139:7-12 (only a portion is printed below)

> *"Where can I go from Your Spirit?*
> *Or where can I flee from Your presence?...*
> *Indeed, the darkness shall not hide from You,*
> *But the night shines as the day;*
> *The darkness and the light are both alike to You."*

e. **Jeremiah 23:23-24**

> *"'Am I a God near at hand,' says the LORD,*
> *'And not a God afar off? Can anyone hide himself*
> *in secret places, so I shall not see him?' says the LORD;*
> *'Do I not fill heaven and earth?' says the LORD."*

f. Matthew 28:20

> *"...lo, I am with you always, even to the end of the age."*

7. Spend some time meditating on the verses from Psalm 46 which began this lesson:

> *"God is our refuge and strength, a very present help in trouble.*
> *Therefore we will not fear, even though the earth be removed,*
> *And though the mountains be carried into the midst of the sea;*
> *Though its waters roar and be troubled,*
> *Though the mountains shake with its swelling...*
>
> *The LORD of hosts is with us; the God of Jacob is our refuge."*

What thought stands out most as you consider these truths?

8. The psalmists knew the character and promises of God. Even when they could not sense His presence, they knew He was there and that they could expect an answer. Consider the hope that the following passage displays. Would you make this prayer of David's your own prayer today?   If so, pray it now and then initial the box.

> *"Answer me speedily, O LORD;*
> *My spirit fails!...*
> *Cause me to hear Your lovingkindness in the morning,*
> *For in You do I trust;*
> *Cause me to know the way in which I should walk,*
> *For I lift up my soul to You."*
> Psalm 143:7-8

28

Understanding Biblical Hope

*W*hy is hope so important? The following passage expresses one reason in an analogy. Underline the phrase which tells what a man with hope in God is like.

> *"Blessed is the man...whose hope is in the LORD.*
> *He shall be like a tree planted by the waters, which spreads out its roots by the river,*
> *and will not fear when heat comes;*
> *But its leaf will be green, and will not be anxious in the year of drought,*
> *nor will cease from yielding fruit."*
>
> Jeremiah 17:7-8

We live in a fallen, sinful world, and so we will all have trouble and disappointments. Every person experiences difficulty and hardship. Every person has "down" days and times of sorrow. Yet during these times of "drought," we can still yield fruit (have lives that are productive, useful and godly) if we hope in the LORD. Hope in the LORD is the essential thing which will see us through days of sorrow and trouble.

God has not left us alone to blindly discover on our own the truths we need to know about hope. Instead, through His Spirit, He has given His Word with rich teachings on this subject. In this study, you will examine some of these precious, essential truths.

1. Below you will find some of the words translated "hope" in the Old Testament (Hebrew) and New Testament (Greek). A brief definition of each word is given. The Strong's reference numbers[1] are in parentheses should you wish to complete a more extensive word study.

Old Testament (Hebrew):

  a. tiqvah (#8615)   *expectancy: expectation*

  b. tocheleth (#8431)   *expectation: hope*

  c. yachal (#3176)   *root: to wait; by implication to be patient, hope, tarry, trust*

New Testament (Greek):

  d. elpis (#1680)   *root: to anticipate, usually with pleasure; expectation or confidence, faith*

From these definitions, how would you describe the difference between biblical hope and the world's idea of hope (an uncertain "I hope so, but can't count on it" attitude)?

2. Some important questions about hope are listed below. As you read the verses in the left hand column, circle the word "hope" each time you see it. Then, in the right hand column, briefly record each passage's answer to the question. *(Some are completed for you.)*

a. Verses	In whom or what am I to place my hope?
And now, Lord, what do I wait for? My hope is in You. Psalm 39:7	the Lord
Paul, an apostle of Jesus Christ, by the commandment of God our Savior and the Lord Jesus Christ, our hope. 1 Timothy 1:1	
My soul faints for Your salvation, But I hope in Your word...You are my hiding place and my shield; I hope in Your word. Psalm 119:81, 114	
Behold, the eye of the LORD is on those who fear Him, on those who hope in His mercy... Psalm 33:18a	
...in hope of eternal life which God, who cannot lie, promised before time began... Titus 1:2	
...rest your hope fully upon the grace that is to be brought to you at the revelation of Jesus Christ. 1 Peter 1:13	

What are some things that people tend to hope in other than God, His Word and His work?

b. Verses	Why do I need hope?
Be of good courage, and He shall strengthen your heart, All you who hope in the LORD. Psalm 31:24	for courage & strength of heart
...rejoicing in hope... Romans 12:12a	it brings joy
But I do not want you to be ignorant, brethren, concerning those who have fallen asleep, lest you sorrow as others who have no hope. 1 Thessalonians 4:13	
But sanctify the Lord God in your hearts, and always be ready to give a defense to everyone who asks you a reason for the hope that is in you... 1 Peter 3:15	to increase opportunities to tell others about Christ

Verses *(continued)*   **Why do I need hope?**

And everyone who has this hope in Him purifies himself,
just as He is pure. 1 John 3:3

This hope we have as an anchor of the soul, both sure and
steadfast... Hebrews 6:19

Sum up the need for and benefits of having hope in God: which areas of life does hope impact?

---

c. Verses   **How do I get this hope?**

Now may our Lord Jesus Christ Himself, and our God
and Father, who has loved us and given us everlasting
consolation and good hope by grace...   2 Thessalonians 2:16

...who according to His abundant mercy has begotten us   begotten (born) again to it by God
again to a living hope through the resurrection of Jesus
Christ from the dead, to an inheritance...reserved in
heaven for you, who are kept by the power of God
through faith...   1 Peter 1:3-5

For whatever things were written before were written for
our learning, that we through the patience and comfort of
the Scriptures might have hope. Romans 15:4

...that you may abound in hope by the power of the Holy
Spirit. Romans 5:13

Thoughts on how to gain true hope

---

d. Verses

Hope is a gift from God, but do I have any responsibility to get or maintain it?

...at that time you were without Christ...having no hope and without God in the world. But now in Christ Jesus you who once were far off have been brought near by the blood of Christ. Ephesians 2:12-13

be sure Jesus Christ is my Lord and Savior

My soul, wait silently for God alone, For my expectation [hope] is from Him. He only is my rock and my salvation; He is my defense; I shall not be moved. Psalm 62:5

But I will hope continually, and will praise You yet more and more. Psalm 71:14

[Paul praying for the Ephesian believers] that you may know what is the hope of His calling... Ephesians 1:18

pray for it

...continue in the faith, grounded and steadfast... not moved away from the hope of the gospel which you heard... Colossians 1:23

For whatever things were written before were written for our learning, that we through the patience and comfort of the Scriptures might have hope. Romans 15:4

Therefore we do not lose heart...For our light affliction, which is but for a moment, is working for us a far more exceeding and eternal weight of glory...For I consider that the sufferings of this present time are not worthy to be compared with the glory which shall be revealed in us... For we were saved in this hope...we eagerly wait for it with perseverance. 2 Corinthians 4:16-18 and Romans 8:18-25

don't lose heart

think biblically about suffering

eagerly wait with perseverance

How well are you fulfilling your responsibilities in the area of hope? Which area(s) of responsibility are the hardest to fulfill in times of depression? What could help?

3. God uses three objects to describe the importance of hope in our lives today. As you study the following verses, think about how these objects picture the nature and work of hope. Record what you learn and add additional thoughts that come to mind. If you are artistically inclined, feel free to draw pictures!

a. Hebrews 6:18-19 compares hope to what nautical object? _____

    1) What does an anchor do? What are its uses?

    2) How does this give an understanding of biblical hope?

b. 1 Thessalonians 5:8 describes hope as a _____.

    1) What does a helmet do? What are its uses? *(List as many as possible.)*

    2) How does this give an understanding of hope?

c. The third picture is from Jeremiah 17:7-8, which is quoted at the beginning of this lesson. It tells us that a man who has the LORD as his hope is like a _____
_____.

    1) List at least three characteristics of this tree:

    2) What part of this description most appeals to you? Why?

4. What is one truth from this study that you could use to begin to encourage a friend who is having trouble maintaining hope?

$5.$ The final questions for today are:

_____ Do you desire to have greater and greater hope?

_____ Have you done the "first thing" by placing your faith in Jesus Christ as Lord and Savior?

_____ Are you willing to do your part in developing, strengthening and maintaining your hope?

_____ Do you see the tribulations of your life as a means of producing hope? Have you thanked God for these opportunities?

_____ If your hope is strong, are you willing to help those who are weak in hope to trust in God?

_____ Will you stay consistently in God's Word so that you will be prepared to give an answer for the hope that is in you?

End your study in a time of prayer and commitment. When you finish, initial the box.

Thoughts, Meditations and Prayers

Hear my cry, O God;
Attend to my prayer.
From the end of the earth I will cry to You,

When my heart is overwhelmed;
Lead me to the rock that is higher than I.

For You have been a shelter for me,
A strong tower from the enemy.

I will abide in Your tabernacle forever;
I will trust in the shelter of Your wings.

Psalm 61:1-4

Lesson Two

How Long, Lord?

"Those who wait on the LORD...
shall mount up with wings like eagles..."
Isaiah 40:31

*W*hen my children were young, our family often vacationed at my parents' house. About the time my daughter, Amy, turned two years old, one of her favorite things to do while we were there was to wait for her grandfather (she calls him Da) to come home from work.

My parents' house is situated at the top of a hill, and Amy would stand with my mother (her grandmother) on the large, brick porch so that she could see down the road to the first curve. With each car that passed, Amy would perk up just a bit. When it wasn't Da's car, she would lean back against her grandmother, but her eyes remained on the road, ready for him to come around the bend. When he finally arrived, she would wave as the car went by, clamber off the porch, run down the sidewalk with her arms out and greet him with a big hug.

Usually, Da arrived within two to five minutes of Amy and my mom going out to the porch. On one day, though, Da was almost 45 minutes late. It was in the days before cell phones, and after a while, Mom and I began whispering to each other: "What do you think happened?" "Surely he would have called if he had to work late." "Do you think there was an accident?" All kinds of things went through our heads. Eventually, Mom suggested that we all go inside to wait, but Amy sweetly protested, saying that she knew

Da would be home any minute and she didn't want to miss him. The three of us remained on the porch, but only Amy waited without any doubt at all.

The faith of a child is precious. We often hear that, to be saved, one must become as a little child: humble and without anything to offer in return (Matthew 18:2-4). I think it is equally important that we maintain the faith of a child when it comes to trust and hope in God.

My mom and I were not wrong to wonder whether anything had happened to my dad. Dad is human. He was, indeed, late (due to bad traffic and an unexpected stop at a plant and garden sale where he lost track of time).

However, God is not human as we are. He is eternal. He is all-powerful. He never loses track of time. His plans can never be thwarted...and He will NEVER be late. Knowing all this (and so much more!) about God, we must be like a trusting child when life is not as we would like or expect it to be. We must continually, expectantly wait for our Father's help. If it does not seem to come immediately, or on our timetable, we must wait with patience and anticipation. Da had told Amy that he would see her after work, and she believed him with all of her heart. God has given us as His children much greater and more precious promises that we can live by every day.

When Da finally arrived, Amy's excitement at seeing him made up for every minute of waiting. When the Lord brings deliverance, our joy will be full and complete, as well.

Today, is your heart "on the porch," expectantly waiting? Will you continue waiting until you see His promises fulfilled?*

Eternal Father,

As I am in Your Word, give me patient endurance
and greater hope in You!

*Appendix B contains photographs of Amy waiting on the porch and greeting Da. Is this what your heart looks like?

PART ONE

> *"Hear _____ _____ , O God; Attend to my prayer.*
> *From the end of the earth ___ _____ _____ to You..."*
> Psalm 61:1-2a

$\mathcal{J}$eremiah was both a priest and a prophet in Old Testament times. His ministry was mostly one of warning the people of Judah that they faced impending captivity. The people did not listen. Instead, Jeremiah was thrown into a pit, publicly humiliated, persecuted by his own family, forced to flee, put in confinement, flogged, threatened, ignored and ridiculed. His people's hardness of heart caused Jeremiah profound sorrow: so much so that he became known as "the weeping prophet." Some of his laments ("loud cries") are recorded in the book of Lamentations.

1. Begin by looking briefly at one of Jeremiah's episodes of depression.

   a. Read Lamentations 3:1-18. (Lamentations is located directly after the book of Jeremiah.) As you read, record at least **nine phrases that show the depth of depression** that Jeremiah was experiencing. Place a check mark beside any entry that includes thoughts and emotions that you, too, have experienced. The first one is completed for you.

     1) 3:_1_   *I am the man who has seen affliction* _____

     2) 3:___   _____

     3) 3:___   _____

     4) 3:___   _____

     5) 3:___   _____

     6) 3:___   _____

     7) 3:___   _____

     8) 3:___   _____

     9) 3:___   _____

   b. How many check marks did you place above?

2. Jeremiah's depression included feelings of being alone, abandoned by God, trapped, helpless, bitter, victimized, in darkness, confused, unsure and miserable. How did he respond to his feelings of depression? Did he allow himself to go deeper into them, or did he fight back? Did he live by what he was feeling, or by what he knew? You decide as you study.

Response #1... Lamentations 3:21
> He reasons with himself. The things that he tells himself are in the following verses, but for now, record the result that calling these things to mind had on his depression.

Response #2... Lamentations 3:22-23
> He thinks on the character of God.
>
> *a.* Find three words in these verses that give insight into God's character, and write them below.
>
> *b.* These are wonderful verses. Choose one phrase to write out in the space below.

Response #3... Lamentations 3:24
> He reminds himself of God's ability to meet his needs. What does he say to himself in his soul?

Response #4... Lamentations 3:25-26
> He acknowledges that he has responsibilities in light of God's character and God's promises.
>
> *a.* List one promise and at least two responsibilities found in these verses.
>
> *Promises*   *Responsibilities*
>
> *b.* In your list, underline the responsibility to wait on the LORD.

3. So what did you decide? Was Jeremiah in a downward spiral with no hope, or was he waiting with a sure expectation that the LORD would bring deliverance?

How about you?

PART TWO

> "Hear my cry, O _____ ; Attend to my prayer.
> From the _____ of the _____ I will cry to _____ ..."
> Psalm 61:1-2a

*G*od chose to record many instances of depression for us in Scripture. We are never alone in our feelings and experiences! Today, learn more from the psalmist Asaph.

1. Asaph expresses feelings of depression in Psalm 77; however, he does not explain why he is so troubled.

   a. Read Psalm 77:1-3 and sum up Asaph's feelings and actions.

   b. How many questions does he ask himself in verses 6-9?

   c. Write out at least two of these questions using your own words.

   d. Do you think believers commonly ask such questions? Why or why not?

2. Now compare Asaph's response in Psalm 77 with Jeremiah's response in Lamentations.

   a. Which words in verses 10-12 are similar to Jeremiah's words, "this I recall to mind" (Lamentations 3:21)?

   b. Compare verses 13-15 with Lamentations 3:22-26. What do their thoughts have in common?

3. As you think about the main ideas from these first two lessons, especially note that godly men took an active approach to dealing with their depression. They talked to, reasoned with and examined themselves. In other words, as they waited on the LORD, they controlled their thoughts, and they constantly infused their mind with biblical truth about God, His mighty works and His past goodness.

One of the biggest problems with depression is that there is a strong tendency to *listen to self* rather than to *reason with self* from Scripture. By listening to self, we can (often unwittingly) tell ourselves things which, although they are based on real feelings, experiences, circumstances, etc., are actually contrary to God's Word.

> *"The heart is deceitful above all things,*
> *and desperately wicked; who can know it?"*
> Jeremiah 17:9

The psalmists and Jeremiah recognized their feelings and circumstances; however, rather than listen to themselves and think on their misery, they reasoned with themselves. Jeremiah said, "This I recall to mind, therefore I have hope." (Lam. 3:21) Asaph said, "I will remember...I will also meditate..." (Psalm 77:11-12)

Spend some time now recalling past instances of the LORD's faithfulness, love, and compassion toward you. This may be difficult if you are currently experiencing feelings of depression, so I have started a list for you. Read over the given entries and then add as many more as you can.

I See the LORD's Faithfulness to Me When I Recall...

The sun that shines without fail (though sometimes clouds hide it)
The physical shelter that God has provided to shield me from heat, cold, and storms
Food that nourishes my body
   You continue the list...

4. There is one last thing to add to your list (if it is not already there!) and that is "the gift of God's Word." Have you considered the fact that God does not "owe" humanity anything, including knowledge of Himself? He has graciously chosen to make Himself known through His Word and to use it for our good.

In the passages below, underline each work that God's Word (precepts) accomplishes, and then circle the responses believers should have to that work.

> *"He sent His word and healed them, and delivered them from their destructions.*
> *Oh, that men would give thanks to the LORD for His goodness."*
> Psalm 107:20-21

> *"I will never forget your precepts, for by them You have given me life...*
> *Through your precepts I get understanding;*
> *Therefore I hate every false way."*
> Psalm 119:93, 104

42

5. In Psalm 119:36, the psalmist pleads:

"Incline my heart to Your testimonies..."

Will you make this your prayer today? Will you ask God to incline your heart more and more to His Word? It may have been a long time since you loved spending time in Bible study. You may never have loved it. But now, sincerely ask that God would cause you to long for His Word.

Will you also ask Him to revive you as you walk in His way and to give light as you read His Word? After you do this, initial the box below. If you feel you cannot pray this prayer at this time, write down why you will not do so.

```
┌──────────┐
│          │
│          │
└──────────┘
```

PART THREE

> *"_____ my cry, O God; _____ to my prayer.*
> *_____ the end of the earth ____ _____ cry _____ _____..."*
> Psalm 61:1-2a

*T*here is still much to learn about waiting for God to deliver, heal and increase hope. Do you remember Jeremiah's words about waiting for the LORD? Circle the word "wait" each time you see it in the verses below.

> *"The LORD is good to them who wait for Him,*
> *To the soul who seeks Him.*
> *It is good that one should hope and wait quietly*
> *For the salvation of the LORD."*
> Lamentations 3:25-26

Even in his depression, Jeremiah had a sure and certain hope that God would hear and answer his prayers.

God's people are waiting for the day when He will fulfill all of His promises and wipe away every tear from their eyes—a day when there will be no more sorrow (Revelation 21:4).

A song is prepared for this day, and when all waiting is over, God's people will sing it. It is a most wonderful and instructive song, a song of hope, a song that tells the reward of waiting on God, a song "...written for the support and assistance of the faith and hope of God's people in all ages..."[1]

1. This song is recorded in Isaiah 26. Focus on only two portions of this song: verses 1-4 and 8-9.

   a. Record the two conditions for perfect peace. (v. 3)

   b. By what names does verse 4 refer to God?

   c. As the people waited for the LORD, what two main desires did they have? (v. 8)

      1) Re-write these two desires using your own words.

      2) Would a believer ever be justified in putting personal or independent desires above the desire to glorify and remember God's name? Why or why not?

   d. According to verse 9, when did the people desire and seek God?

   e. What did they ultimately learn? (end of v. 9)

2. *(Optional)* Using comparison and scriptural reasoning, consider: because God's promises (for both this life and the life to come) are so sure, we can begin thanking Him now for what He will do in the future. Matthew Henry says it this way:

> "...we must be forward to meet God with our thanksgivings
> when he is coming towards us with his mercies."[2]

God's faithfulness to His promises is so certain that, following the example of the song in Isaiah 26, we can also prepare a song to sing in the day when perfect peace is ours.

   a. Choose at least one phrase from Isaiah 26:3-4 and 8-9 that you would like to be a part of your song in the day your deliverance comes. Write the phrase(s) below.

   b. Why did you choose those words for your song?

3. As you read and think on the following thoughts about the future, circle the word "but," and underline the contrast.

> *"Sing praise to the LORD, you saints of His,*
> *And give thanks at the remembrance of His holy name...*
> *Weeping may endure for a night, but joy comes in the morning."*
>
> Psalm 30:4-5

4. The promises of God are sure! If you are His child, you have a song to sing! Although you do not know when it will come, you can count on deliverance as a sure thing as you wait for the LORD! Read the following verses out loud, underlining any portions that stand out to you as you read.

> *"Oh, magnify the LORD with me and let us exalt His name together.*
> *I sought the LORD, and He heard me,*
> *And delivered me from all my fears...*
> *The righteous cry out, and the LORD hears,*
> *And delivers them out of all their troubles...*
> *Many are the afflictions of the righteous, but the LORD delivers him out of them all."*
>
> Psalm 34:3-4, 17, 19

End your study time with prayer as you look forward to that day! Even if it seems impossible to you at this time, thank Him that joy will come and that you will have a song to sing. Initial the box when you are finished.

Note: If you are not currently completing the topical studies along with this foundation lesson, take time to complete the first three pages of Topic Two (*When God Says "Wait"*) before going on to the next lesson. The truths there are essential to keep in mind.

Thought for meditation:

Psalm 123:1-2 says:

> *"Unto You I lift up my eyes,*
> *O You who dwell in the heavens.*
> *Behold, as the eyes of servants look to the hand of their masters,*
> *As the eyes of a maid to the hand of her mistress,*
> *So our eyes look to the LORD our God..."*

As you wait for deliverance (or any other promise to be fulfilled), do your eyes look up to the LORD or down in gloom, sadness and despair?

If they look up, do they look up humbly—as the eyes of a servant to a Master? If not, or if not consistently, will you ask God to humble you and cause you to see Him as the only Master and LORD of your life?

Thoughts, Meditations and Prayers

El Olam The Everlasting God

As a believer, how can you know for certain that deliverance will come? How can you trust God's promises day after day, week after week, year after year and generation after generation? What if God's plans change? What if He doesn't come through?

In other words: On what basis can you trust God's promises enough to wait on Him until He answers?

The name El (or Elohim) Olam is one basis. Our God is the Everlasting God—and the implications of this name are awesome!

El is a word which emphasizes might and appears many times throughout the Old Testament, often in the names of God. Elohim is the most common Hebrew word that English Bibles translate as "God."

Olam means "hidden" or "concealed."

> *"...the word 'Olam'...contains in itself both the idea of a 'secret,'*
> *and also of 'time,' or of 'an age.'...*
> *Hence it came to mean 'time hidden from man,' or 'time indefinite.'...*
> *'El Olam' is the 'Age-God,' or 'God of the Ages,'*
> *that is, the God who works His will, not all at once, but through successive times."* [1]

In other words, the LORD is not limited to the present. Rather, He is the God of all ages—past, present and future.

1. Read Isaiah 40:25-31. The name Elohim Olam (Everlasting God) appears near the middle of the passage. Don't miss it!

   a. Verses 25-26 tell men to observe the stars in the heavens. Why do you think God wants man to take notice of them? What do they tell and show about God? *(If needed, see Psalm 19:1 and Romans 1:20)*

   b. After calling people to lift up their eyes and see the heavens, God asks a question.

      1) Read verse 27 (in more than one translation, if possible).

      2) One commentary states, "The language used here suggests that the people were bringing God down to their own level, thinking him either forgetful...or tired—perhaps because their long history of folly seemed to be never-ending." [2] Do you see this attitude today? If so, how?

c. To help correct their thought patterns, God calls on His people to examine what they know and then reminds them of who He is. Read verse 28 out loud.

    1) Write out the two questions at the beginning of verse 28.

    2) Record at least two things God says about Himself in the rest of this verse.

d. As you read verses 29-30,

    1) List or summarize the claims/promises.

    2) Note the condition for renewed strength. *(v. 31...use more than one translation, if possible)*

2. The eternal nature of God is often connected not only to His mighty power, but also to His understanding and wisdom.

    a. In the passages below, underline words and phrases that relate to God's power and/or wisdom.

> *"The **everlasting God**...Neither faints nor is weary. His understanding is unsearchable."*
> Isaiah 40:28

> *"...I am God, and there is none like Me, declaring the end from the beginning,*
> *And **from ancient times** things that are not yet done...Indeed I have spoken it; I will also bring it to pass..."*
> Isaiah 46:9-11

> *"But the LORD is the true God;*
> *He is the living God and the **everlasting King**...*
> *He has made the earth by His power, He has established the world by His wisdom..."*
> Jeremiah 10:10-12

> *"Now to the **King eternal**, immortal, invisible, to God who alone is wise,*
> *be honor and glory forever and ever. Amen."*
> I Timothy 1:17

    b. God's wise purposes and plans for His people transcend the present. He encompasses these within His plans for all eternity. He doesn't act based only on today, or only on one person, but always in light of all He knows and plans for all times. (Sometimes that means we, who are bound by time, will have to wait without fully understanding why.)

    And don't fail to make the connection between the Everlasting God and the length of time He has loved His people:

> *"...I have loved you with an **everlasting love**..."*
> Jeremiah 31:3

Spend a few moments meditating on *that* thought before you go on!

3. So...because El Olam is able to see the past, present and future, and

　　because He alone possesses power great enough to uphold the universe, and

　　because He alone is wise with an eternal and unchanging wisdom, and

　　because He has loved His people with an everlasting love...

would it not reasonably follow that His long-loved people should have total trust, faith and hope in His ways and timing, especially when He says such things as:

"'...I know the plans I have for you,' declares the LORD, 'plans to prosper you and not to harm you, plans to give you hope and a future.'"

Jeremiah 29:11 NIV

"...God is faithful, who will not allow you to be tempted beyond what you are able, but with the temptation will also make the way of escape, that you may be able to bear it."

1 Corinthians 10:13

"Many are the afflictions of the righteous, but the LORD delivers him out of them all."

Psalm 34:19

There is a difference, however, between understanding or acknowledging something as truth and really living in light of it, but acknowledgment is the first step!   For the three verses just quoted:

a. Mark an "A" in the margin beside the verses you understand to be truth and *acknowledge* as being something you should live in light of.

b. Write "LILOI" (Living **I**n **L**ight **O**f **I**t) beside those which you *do* consistently live in light of.

4. Read or sing the words to the hymn *O God, Our Help in Ages Past.*

O God, our help in ages past, Our hope for years to come,
Our shelter from the stormy blast, And our eternal home.

Before the hills in order stood, Or earth received her frame,
From everlasting Thou art God, To endless years the same.

A thousand ages in Thy sight Are like an evening gone;
Short as the watch that ends the night, Before the rising sun.

O God, our help in ages past, Our hope for years to come,
Be Thou our guard while life shall last, And our eternal home.[3]

5. In Isaiah 40:26, God told the people to *"lift up your eyes on high and see who has created these things..."* These are wise instructions for today, too. Go to your window now and look outside. Take a few minutes to ponder the **Everlasting God** that creation shows forth. Think about the wonder of how all the stars, planets, trees, flowers, rain, snow, rivers, sand, oceans and animals came into being. Try to fathom, just a little, the might and wisdom that it took to create all of nature—and then think on the power and wisdom it takes to uphold it. Go now, and stay a while at your window. Think about God and how powerful, awesome, and eternal He is. Then come back.

6. What is the main thought that has come to mind as you studied the name El Olam?

7. *(Optional)* If you would like to study other references which contain this name, they are: Genesis 21:33, Psalm 90:2, Isaiah 63:16, Micah 5:2, and Romans 16:26. Make any notes on a separate sheet of paper.

8. Would you pray the prayer below, or one of your own? Initial the box when you are finished.

> *LORD*, You are El Olam, the Everlasting God, and You have always known that today I would study Your name and then respond in prayer. Thank You for bringing me to Your Word today.
>
> I am so grateful that You see the "big picture" and that You work out every detail in light of Your holy and wise purposes. Please bring Your name, El Olam, to my mind whenever I begin to doubt Your ways or become impatient with Your timing. Help me grow in my understanding of Your eternal nature, power and wisdom, and help me begin to live more consistently in light of what I do comprehend.
>
> LORD, it is so mind-boggling and humbling that You, the Everlasting God, have loved Your people from everlasting! It is so comforting to know that You have loved me for that long! Thank You for loving me. I desire to be as faithful in my love for You as You have been to me. May I show my love for You, and trust in You, more and more for all eternity!

When God Says "Wait"

"And now, Lord, what do I wait for? My hope is in You."
Psalm 39:7

*D*eliverance from our trials is one of the things for which we most long. Examining some of the LORD's marvelous acts of deliverance reveals that His people were not all delivered in the same way or in the same time frame: some of His people had immediate deliverance, and others had to wait for days, years, even decades.

1. For each of the following individuals or groups, record the different means of deliverance that God used, and give the approximate time each of them had to wait before they were delivered from their trial or distress.

   a. Daniel's deliverance from the lions in the lion's den (Daniel 6:16-23)
   How delivered:
   Time he had to wait before the LORD closed their mouths:

   b. Paul and Silas from the angry mob and prison (Acts 16:22-40)
   How delivered:
   Time they had to wait for freedom:

   c. The beggar from blindness (John 9:1-11)
   How delivered:
   His waiting time must have been at least:

   d. The children of Israel from bondage in Egypt (Exodus 12:40-41, 14:21-31; Psalm 77:17-19)
   How delivered: *(There could be many parts to this answer; however, be sure to include how they were ultimately delivered when Pharaoh's army gave chase!)*

   Time they had to wait before freedom:

2. *(Optional)* What are other ways God chose to deliver His people from their trials (and how long did they have to wait)?

3. Consider the following:

Why are some people delivered immediately and others only after years of hardship?

Is God distracted? Unfeeling? Uncaring? Unjust?

Why are there so many different ways and means of deliverance?

Why are some of these awe-inspiring and miraculous and others seemingly more normal?

What are God's purposes?

Underline answers you learn from the following verses and then sum up your findings in the box provided:

God's Purposes for His Various Acts of Deliverance Include...

a. Psalm 78:4-8 *(Only verses 6-7 are written below. If you have time, read the entire passage.)*

"That the generation to come might know them [the works, strength, etc. of the LORD],
the children who would be born, that they may arise and declare them to their children,
that they may set their hope in God, and not forget the works of God, but keep His commandments"

b. Psalm 105:1-5

"Oh, give thanks to the LORD! Call upon His name; make known His deeds among the peoples!
Sing to Him, sing psalms to Him; talk of all His wondrous works! Glory in His holy name;
let the hearts of those rejoice who seek the LORD! Seek the LORD and His strength;
seek His face evermore! Remember His marvelous works which He has done,
His wonders, and the judgments of His mouth"

c. John 9:1-3

"Now as Jesus passed by, He saw a man who was blind from birth.
And His disciples asked Him, saying, 'Rabbi, who sinned, this man or his parents,
that he was born blind?' Jesus answered, 'Neither this man nor his parents sinned,
but that the works of God should be revealed in him.'"

d. John 20:30-31

"And truly Jesus did many other signs in the presence of His disciples, which are not written
in this book, but these are written that you may believe that Jesus is the Christ, the Son of God,
and that believing you may have life in His name."

In summary, God has various ways, means and times of deliverance because He uses them...

4. Having considered your God and His mighty works of deliverance, use reason and faith (and Scripture—some example references are provided) to answer the following questions:

   a. Is there anything too hard for your God? (Jeremiah 32:16-17, 26-27)

   b. Could He deliver you in this very instant if He so chose? (Psalm 33:8-9)

   c. Would He withhold help and deliverance without a purpose? (Jeremiah 29:11)

   d. Will anything He does ever be for your ultimate harm or detriment? (Romans 8:28-29)

   e. Will you always know or understand His ways or timing? (Isaiah 55:8-9, Deuteronomy 29:29)

   f. Will He ever let it all be too much for you to bear? (1 Corinthians 10:13)

5. A definition of biblical waiting is:
   to expect, await, look for patiently, hope; to be confident, trust; to be enduring. [2]

Complete the following sentence by using your own words to explain the meaning of the word "wait."

   When someone waits for the LORD, there will be...

4. Having considered your God and His mighty works of deliverance, use reason and faith (and Scripture—some example references are provided) to answer the following questions:

   a. Is there anything too hard for your God? (Jeremiah 32:16-17, 26-27)

How to Wait on the LORD

	Principle	Specific Application
a. Psalm 119:28 *(see also Luke 4:4)* *"My soul melts from heaviness; strengthen me according to Your word."*	Stay in God's Word	Complete studies with at least one other person so I won't be as likely to let time in God's Word diminish.
b. 1 Thessalonians 5:17 *"Pray without ceasing,"*		When praying seems difficult, read a hymn or a psalm and use those words as my own prayer.
c. Hebrews 10:25 *"not forsaking the assembling of ourselves together, as is the manner of some..."*		Attend church services whether I feel like it or not, and be involved in a small group where I can fellowship with other believers.
d. Ecclesiastes 4:9-12 *"Two are better than one...For if they fall, one will lift up his companion, But woe to him who is alone when he falls, For he has no one to help him up..."*	Help others and accept help	
e. Proverbs 20:18 *(See also Proverbs 15:22)* *"Plans are established by counsel; By wise counsel wage war."*	Seek wise counsel	

f. **Colossians 3:2-4** *Principle* *Specific Application*
  (see also Hebrews 11:10, 13, 27; 12:2)

"*Set your mind on things above, not on things on the earth...*" Live now in light of heavenly realities

---

g. **Acts 16:25** *Principle* *Specific Application*
  (the psalmists are also examples of this!)

"*[While in prison] Paul and Silas were praying and singing hymns to God...*" | | Spend thirty minutes every morning at 9:00 listening and singing along to well-known hymns or Scripture-based songs.

---

h. **Philippians 2:3-4** *Principle* *Specific Application*

"*...let each esteem others better than himself. Let each look out not only for his own interests, but also for the interests of others.*" Be "others" focused instead of "self" focused

---

i. **1 Peter 1:13-16** *Principle* *Specific Application*

"*Therefore gird up the loins of your mind, be sober...as obedient children, not conforming yourselves to the former lusts...*" | | I will ask my spouse or a godly friend to let me know of one specific area where I need to work on fully obeying God. I will ask him or her to hold me accountable for one week.

---

j. **Psalm 9:10a** *Principle* *Specific Application*

"*And those who know Your name will put their trust in You;*" | | I will complete the study on the names of God in this book and then get another book on His names for ongoing study.

---

k. **1 Timothy 4:8a** *Principle* *Specific Application*
  (see also

"*For bodily exercise profits a little...*" Get or keep active (as much as possible) I will make my bed *first* thing *every* morning so that it will not be so easy or tempting to get back into it.

7. Put a check mark by the principle in Question 6 that you have followed best, and circle the one that needs the most improvement.

How and when will you begin working to improve the area you circled?

8. As you saw at the beginning of this lesson, God's deliverance is sure, but His timing and means can vary widely. You have seen that waiting is not simply "hanging out." Rather, it involves focused activity on your part. You have also seen that we are not to "go it alone." God commands us to help one another through the rough times of life.

There is one final area of importance to consider: how long must you be prepared to wait? Psalm 123:1-2 answers this question.   Read this passage out loud and then fill in the box below.

"Unto You I lift up my eyes,
O You who dwell in the heavens.
Behold, as the eyes of servants look to the hand of their masters,
As the eyes of a maid to the hand of her mistress,
So our eyes look to the LORD our God,
Until He has mercy on us."

> As I wait on the LORD as a servant
> looks to his master, I must be
> prepared to wait for this long:

9. Do you consider your life as belonging to you or to God? If it is God's, then when He calls on you to wait, will you remember that:

> He doesn't have you wait without a reason
>
> He has given you responsibilities to fulfill in the mean time
>
> He will always make sure the waiting works for your good and His glory
>
> The waiting will never be more than you can bear
>
> Your hope is in the Lord—not in the thing or event you desire

and, with His help, will you humbly and faithfully wait "until"? If so, initial the box.

56

Thoughts, Meditations and Prayers

Hear my cry, O God;
Attend to my prayer.

From the end of the earth I will cry to You,
When my heart is overwhelmed;
Lead me to the rock that is higher than I.

For You have been a shelter for me,
A strong tower from the enemy.

I will abide in Your tabernacle forever;
I will trust in the shelter of Your wings.

Psalm 61:1-4

Lesson Three

The Word of Truth

"For the commandment is a lamp, and the law a light;
Reproofs of instruction are the way of life"

Proverbs 6:23

I'm a city girl, through and through. However, I do have wonderful memories of living just a ways out into the country. As we were house-hunting before a move to Alabama, we came upon a house that we loved (and would later call home) in a small community near Montgomery known as Emerald Mountain. We first toured the house in the evening, and when we came back outside, it was a lovely night: dark and peaceful, with only a slight breeze. As we walked down the driveway to our car, one of us happened to look up. Soon, we were all looking.

The sky was beautiful. It was dark, but we could clearly see multitudes of stars...many more stars than we had been able to see from our "city houses." We stood, faces up, for quite a while as we marveled at God's amazing creation.

You can only see stars when it is dark. We city-dwellers don't see nearly as many stars as people in the country do...in fact, we rarely even look up for them because they are so obscured by the man-made lights.

God calls us to lift up our spiritual eyes when we are in times of darkness. Although worldly things may obscure our vision, if we look carefully, we will be able to see His light. Just as those who wait for the sun can still find light from the stars in the dark of night, so you, as you wait for total deliverance and relief, can still find God's love, plan and purposes during a "dark" time.

Do not be discouraged if the light seems far away. Rather, thank Him that He cares for you so much that He sends light (from His Word and His Spirit) for your spiritually dark times as well as the moon and the stars for physical darkness. (Have you ever thought how good and wise it was of God not to leave the night sky without any light at all?)

Whatever your darkness, thank Him for the light that He *has* given—and know that when the full light of day finally comes, you will enjoy it even more!

Creator of All Things,

Lift up my eyes to see Your wondrous works.
Thank You for the light of Your Word;
and thank You that it will always give me enough light to know You and
find the way that I should go.

PART ONE

> *"From the end of the earth I will cry _____ _____ ,*
> *When my _____ is overwhelmed;*
> *Lead me _____ _____ _____ that is higher than I."*
>
> Psalm 61:2

*I*n Lesson Two, you saw that we have a responsibility to live life in light of God's truth. This takes a lifetime to master...but God has promised strength for the journey and ultimate victory. In the midst of hurt, troubles and reality, there is hope as long as there is God. **We must not focus so much on the circumstances of life, but rather, on the God who is over all things.** As we come to know Him and His ways, we will gain understanding, direction, security and hope in the midst of our circumstances— and our lives will change.

Although the thought of change is sometimes disconcerting, the truth is that all of us need to change. Not one of us is perfect.

As our Creator and Maker, **God has determined the means for our life-change**: His Word of Truth (Scripture) empowered by His Spirit.

1. Read 1 Thessalonians 2:13 in the various translations/paraphrases[1] below, noting the differences and similarities in each. Underline the one three-word phrase which occurs in each entry.

   a. *"...the word of God, which also effectively works in you who believe."* NKJV

   b. *"...the word of God, which is at work in you who believe."* NIV

   c. *"...the word of God, which also performs its work in you who believe."* NAS

   d. *"...God's Word, a power in the lives of you who believe."* Phillips

   e. *"...the Word of God, which is effectually at work in you who believe—exercising its [superhuman] power in those who adhere to and trust in and rely on it."* Amplified

2. Since the Spirit of God uses His Word to bring about life-change, what must we know about this Word of Truth? One of the first things to know is what it says about man and man's relationship with God. Let me tell you about what I was taught as a child.

   a. **I was taught that everyone is a sinner, and that sin has separated us from God.** That was and is true, for God's Word says:

> *"There is none righteous, no, not one..."*

> *"...for all have sinned and fall short of the glory of God..."*

> *"For whoever shall keep the whole law, and yet stumble in one point, he is guilty of all."*

> *"But your iniquities have separated you from your God..."*

> Romans 3:10, 23; James 2:10; Isaiah 59:2

Place a star beside any of these verses that are familiar to you.

b. **I was taught that my only hope of being saved from my sins was the forgiveness found only in Jesus Christ and His work on the cross.** Again, that was and is true, for God's Word says:

> *"But when the kindness and the love of God our Savior toward man appeared,*
> *not by works of righteousness which we have done,*
> *but according to His mercy He saved us..."*

> *"Now all things are of God,*
> *who has reconciled us to Himself through Jesus Christ..."*

> *"For He [God] made Him [Christ] who knew no sin to be sin for us,*
> *that we might become the righteousness of God in Him."*

> *"'Sirs, what must I do to be saved?'*
> *So they said, 'Believe on the Lord Jesus Christ, and you will be saved...'"*
>
> Titus 3:4-5; 2 Corinthians 5:18, 21; Acts 16:30-31

In the first passage above, circle the phrase that tells how someone is *not* saved. Then, in all the passages, underline the phrases that tell how someone *is* saved from sin and separation from God.

c. **I was taught that once I had prayed to receive Jesus Christ as my Lord and Savior, I should never doubt my salvation.** That was not *exactly* true. Record what God's Word says in:

1) 2 Peter 1:10

2) 2 Corinthians 13:5

d. While genuine salvation is forever and can never be lost (John 10:27-29; Romans 8:33-39, 11:29; 1 Cor. 1:7-9; Phil. 1:6; 1 Peter1:3-5, Jude 24-25; etc.), there are times in life when we do not feel the assurance of our salvation. In those times, we must ask ourselves whether or not we have ever genuinely repented of our sinful ways and turned to Christ as the only means for salvation. We must make our "call and election sure."

This is what I ask you to do now. This is an easy question if you know for sure that you have never trusted Christ as your Lord and Savior. It is a much harder question if you have thought yourself a Christian for many years.

Are you sure of your salvation? If you say yes, can you point to more than just a time when you
> prayed a prayer,
> walked an aisle,
> filled out a card of commitment or
> participated in a ceremony (baptism, communion, confirmation, etc.)

for assurance that Jesus Christ is your Savior? Take a few minutes and write out below why you believe, do not believe, or are not sure, that you are saved.

(Given the importance of this answer, if you are not sure of your salvation or would like more information on how to be saved, please speak with a pastor, teacher or Christian friend who can explain God's plan of salvation to you.)

3. Why is your relationship with God so important? First, because your eternal destiny rests on it! It is also important because only at salvation does the Holy Spirit enter into a believer's heart...and without the power He provides, biblical life-change is impossible.

> *"And we, who with unveiled faces all reflect the Lord's glory,*
> *are being transformed into his likeness with ever-increasing glory,*
> ***which comes from the Lord, who is the Spirit."***
>
> *"For **it is God who works in you** both to will and to do for His good pleasure."*
>
> 2 Corinthians 3:18 NIV, Philippians 2:13

Your salvation is important because, *without God working in you, with you and for you, all your labor will ultimately be in vain!* You may be able to accomplish some changes and improvements in your own strength, but they will not be God-wrought, permanent, spiritual changes. In fact, you have probably experienced the ups and downs of these "self-improvements" already.

For biblical, God-empowered life-change

a. You must be saved. If you have not trusted Christ as Savior, will you do so now?

- Believe in Jesus Christ who offered Himself on the cross as a sacrifice for your sin. John 5:24

- Repent of your sin and self-centered ways. Ask God for the forgiveness He freely offers. Acts 3:19

- Ask Him to cleanse you and make you a new creation, one who will live wholeheartedly in obedience to His Word. 2 Corinthians 5:17, Psalm 143:8

- Thank Him for the gift of His Holy Spirit, Who will empower you to live in faithfulness to Him and with love for others. Acts 2:38, Galatians 5:22

b. If you are sure that you have already been saved, is your life right with God? Have you moved out of close fellowship with Him? Do you need to repent and turn from sin in your life?

As you begin to examine yourself, consider the list below.
Don't hurry through this; rather, work prayerfully and thoughtfully.
At the end, add any additional thoughts the LORD brings to mind.

Consider the following questions honestly, placing an X by any statements which apply to you. Have you:

_____ Said you love the Lord, but lived independently from His Word?

_____ Spent more time thinking about yourself and your problems than about God and His kingdom?

_____ Looked to others (this includes people as well as things such as food, sleep, work, TV, pills, etc.) for comfort or help before you have looked to the Lord?

_____ Cherished or nurtured a particular sin in your heart?

_____ Turned away from believers who would share God's love and truth with you?

_____ Complained about your circumstances?

_____ Used your past, your family, or others to excuse your present failures?

_____ Allowed your mind to become obsessed with sorrow over a particular fault, decision or action in your past?

_____ Let guilt overwhelm you, rather than deal with it biblically?

_____ Allowed fear and/or anxiety to grow and take control of parts of your life?

_____ Failed to search out biblical help for your depression?

_____ Given up faith or hope in God?

_____ "Tried and tried and tried," but not really persevered?

_____ Neglected to make yourself accountable to a godly discipler?

_____

_____

c. If you put an X beside any of the statements above, then a time of repentance is necessary. Go to your knees (if possible), and tell God the areas where you know you have failed Him and sinned against Him. List your sins specifically, and seek His promised forgiveness...

> *"Have mercy upon me, O God,*
> *According to Your lovingkindness;*
> *According to the multitude of Your tender mercies,*
> *Blot out my transgressions.*
> *Wash me thoroughly from my iniquity,*
> *And cleanse me from my sin.*
>
> Psalm 51:1-2

4. In Part Two, you will look at how to stay in close fellowship with God—even after times of failure. For now, will you make a new or renewed commitment to spending time in God's Word?

PART TWO

> *"From the end of the _____ I will cry to You,*
> *When my heart is _____;*
> *_____ _____ to the rock that is _____ than I."*
> Psalm 61:2

Although it isn't always easy, ongoing self-examination of thoughts, actions and motives is necessary for a believer to stay in close fellowship with God. Time in the Scriptures is essential for this.

However, when depression sets in, it *can* be easy to overlook time in God's Word. There is often just no desire or energy to read or study the Scriptures (a problem which, in and of itself, can produce guilt and deeper depression!). As exposure to God's Word decreases or vanishes, other things also begin to disappear. Two of these are:

Prayer (because true prayer is a response to the truths of God's Word)
Repentance (because God's Word defines sin, and the Holy Spirit uses it to convict us of sin)

Today, the goal is to understand why honest examination, confession and repentance are absolutely essential to overcoming depression.

If you are familiar with the life of King David, you know that he was a believer, a man after God's own heart—who also sinned in grievous ways that impacted his life and family. His sins were many and included adultery, murder, deceit, pride and rebellion against God.

Psalm 51 describes David's sorrow and repentance over his sin. (*Optional:* If you are not familiar with this chapter, read at least the first ten verses now.) In verses 12-13, he asks God,

> *"Restore to me the joy of Your salvation...*
> *Then I will teach transgressors Your ways..."*

In another passage (Psalm 32), David uses his past sin, failure and depression to encourage others to get and stay in a right relationship with God.

1. Read Psalm 32 and note your initial impression(s) along with the verse that stands out most to you.

2. Record what you learn from the instruction and encouragement of Psalm 32.

a. **Psalm 32:1-2**

1) According to these verses, who is blessed?

2) What words in verses 1 and 2 describe disobedience? *(Complete word studies or find definitions in an English dictionary if you have time.)*

3) Record the words which describe the pardon given by God. *(Complete word studies on each if you have time).*

b. **Psalm 32:3-4**

1) What effects did David's unconfessed sin have on his body?

2) Why might God have made it so that our bodies react adversely when sin remains unconfessed? *(Hebrews 12:5-7, 10-11 might help in determining your answer.)*

c. **Psalm 32:5**

1) What actions did David take when confronted with his sin—and what was God's response?

2) Why was this God's response? *(If needed, see 1 John 1:9)*

d. **Psalm 32:6-7**

1) Read these two verses out loud and then notice the "Selah" at the end of verse 7. The word indicates a pause, possibly for reflection and meditation while the instruments continued to play. Spend a couple of minutes contemplating truths you have learned thus far from Psalm 32.

e. **Psalm 32:8-9**

    1) In verse 8, what does God promise He will do?

    2) *(Optional)* Cross-reference His promises with Psalm 119:105. What is the connection?

    3) In Psalm 32:9, what two animals exhibit behaviors that we are to avoid?

    4) What is the main idea behind this analogy? *(You may wish to cross-reference Proverbs 26:3 and James 3:2-3 or consult a commentary.)*

f. **Psalm 32:10-11**

    1) Compare Psalm 32:3-4 with these two verses. What contrasts do you see?

3. As you bring this part of your study to an end, would you make the words of the following hymn your prayer? If, for any reason, you cannot say certain words from your heart, would you tell God that you desire to be able to truly pray these words one day soon? Initial the box when you are finished.

> I am Thine, O Lord, I have heard Thy voice,
> And it told Thy love to me;
> But I long to rise in the arms of faith,
> And be closer drawn to Thee.
>
> Draw me nearer, nearer blessed Lord,
> To the cross where Thou hast died;
> Draw me nearer, nearer, nearer blessed Lord,
> To Thy precious bleeding side.
>
> Consecrate me now, to Thy service, Lord,
> By the pow'r of grace divine;
> Let my soul look up with a steadfast hope,
> And my will be lost in Thine.[2]

PART THREE

> *"From _____ _____ _____ the earth I will cry _____ _____ ,*
> *When _____ _____ is overwhelmed;*
> *Lead me to _____ _____ that _____ _____ than I."*
> Psalm 61:2

$\mathcal{T}$he work of the Word in the life of a believer is so vast and comprehensive that it is almost unbelievable!

Read the following truths about God's Word carefully and thoughtfully...they are essential to overcoming depression and so much more! *This section is a bit longer than some, but spend time here. Don't be concerned if you need more than one study time to complete it all.*

1. Turn to Psalm 119. This is the longest psalm and the longest chapter in the Bible...and has been called the "Mt. Everest of the Psalter." As you look at this psalm, notice that it is divided into 22 sections with each section of eight verses beginning with a different Hebrew letter. It uses many synonyms for "God's Word," some of which are "law," "testimonies," "commandments," "precepts," "judgments" and "statutes."

For each of the 22 sections, I have recorded one way in which that section says the Scripture is powerful in the lives of those who believe. Read each way that Scripture works and each corresponding verse. In six of these sections, I have left out the corresponding verse and put only asterisks (***). In these cases, write out the verse from that section that you think best states the idea on the left.

(Note: Some sections have several verses that apply...simply choose the verse or verses that speak most to you.)

Things every believer can expect from being in the Word of God

Blessings   Section 1 (verses 1-8)

"Blessed are those who keep His testimonies
who seek Him with the whole heart!" v.2

Cleansing and Correction of Both Heart and Life   Section 2 (verses 8-16)

"How can a young man cleanse his way?
By taking heed according to Your word.
Your word I have hidden in my heart,
That I might not sin against You." v. 9, 11

Divine Counsel   Section 3 (verses 17-24)

"Your testimonies also are my delight
And my counselors." v. 24

Strength * ** (your turn!)   Section 4 (verses 25-32)

Power to Walk in Obedience   Section 5 (verses 33-40)

"Make me walk in the path of Your commandments,
For I delight in it." v.35

Freedom   Section 6 (verses 41-48)

"And I will walk about in freedom,
for I have sought out your precepts." v.45 NIV

Hope and Comfort   *   Section 7 (verses 49-56)

Adequacy and Ability to Obey   Section 8 (verses 57-64)

"You are my portion, O LORD;
I have said that I would keep Your words." v. 57

Encouragement in Affliction   Section 9 (verses 65-72)

"Before I was afflicted I went astray, but now I keep Your word."
"It is good for me that I have been afflicted, that I may learn Your statutes." v. 67, 71

69

Things every believer can expect from being in the Word of God (continued)

Tender Mercies (Compassion and Comfort)   Section 10 (verses 73-80)

"Let Your tender mercies come to me, that I may live;
For Your law is my delight." v. 77

Ability to Persevere in Affliction   Section 11 (verses 81-88)

Yet I do not forget Your statutes...All Your commandments are faithful...
Revive me according to Your lovingkindness..." v.83, 86, 88

Security in Uncertain Times ***   Section 12 (verses 89-96)

Understanding and Wisdom   Section 13 (verses 97-104)

"Through Your precepts I get understanding;
Therefore I hate every false way." v.104

Guidance   Section 14 (verses 105-112)

"Your word is a lamp to my feet, And a light to my path...
The wicked have laid a snare for me,
Yet I have not strayed from Your precepts." v.105, 110

Sustaining Power ***   Section 15 (verses 113-120)

Spiritual Discernment   Section 16 (verses 121-128)

"...teach me Your statutes."
"...Give me understanding..." v. 124-125

Insight and Illumination ***   Section 17 (verses 129-136)

Zeal for Righteousness   Section 18 (verses 137-144)

"Your testimonies, which You have commanded, are righteous and very faithful.
My zeal has consumed me, because my enemies have forgotten Your words." v. 138-139

Assurance that God Hears Prayer   Section 19 (verses 145-152)

> *"I cry out with my whole heart...*
> *Hear my voice according to Your lovingkindness...*
> *You are near, O LORD, and all your commandments are truth."* v. 145, 149, 151

Assurance that God is Faithful to Revive and Deliver   Section 20 (verses 153-160)

> *"Consider my affliction and deliver me...Revive me according to Your word...*
> *Revive me, O LORD, according to Your lovingkindness."* v. 153-154, 159

Great Peace *   Section 21 (verses 161-168)

A Heart Full of Worship and Praise   Section 22 (verses 169-176)

> *"My lips shall utter praise, for You teach me Your statutes...*
> *Let my soul live, and it shall praise You."* v. 171, 175

2. Look over all 22 sections from Psalm 119 and place a check mark beside the things you need most in your life today. Then, thank God for what He has promised to those who love Him and are in His Word. Initial the box when you are finished.

Thought for meditation:

A comparison of Colossians 3:16-19 and Ephesians 5:18-21 reveals that a "Spirit-filled life" and a "Word-filled life" have the same results. Thus, the Word of God richly dwelling (being *abundantly* "at home") within the heart and mind is equated to being filled with the Spirit.

An easy way to see this truth is to read down the bolded entries for each of the 22 sections of Psalm 119 above. The list of things which every believer can expect from Scripture also gives a wonderful description of a Spirit-filled (Spirit-controlled) life!

This correlation should not be surprising, since the Scriptures were given by the inspiration, or out-breathing, of God (2 Timothy 3:16) as holy men of God were "moved by the Holy Spirit" (2 Peter 1:21). In fact, the Holy Spirit is so identified with the holy Scriptures that the written Word is called "the sword of the Spirit." (Ephesians 6:17) Further, when Scripture quotes itself, it often says that it is the Spirit speaking (Hebrews 3:7).

Is the Word of God richly at home in your heart, continually filling your thoughts and controlling your actions?

Thoughts, Meditations and Prayers

The Rock

*I*n Psalm 61, David pleads, *"Lead me to the rock that is higher than I."* Salvation and protection in the shipwrecks, tempests and billows of life *must* come from one who is higher than the one lost in the storm. When the waves of life buffet and overwhelm, the cry from every heart must be, "Lead me! It is not within my own strength! Lead me to **the Rock** that is higher than I!"

1. The Hebrew words translated "rock" in the Old Testament can mean a massive boulder or foundation stone, or a cliff or cleft in a mountain.[4] Many passages in Scripture refer to God as the Rock. There is so much to learn about God from these verses. For each entry below, fill in the blanks and record as many truths as possible about God, our "Rock."

a. **Deuteronomy 32:4**, spoken by _____ (see Deuteronomy 31:30)

just before he was to go up Mount _____ (32:49) where he would die (32:44-50).

Truths about God:

b. 1 Samuel 2:2, prayed by _____

Truths about God:

c. **2 Samuel 22:1-4, 31-32, 47** a song by _____ to _____

after the LORD had _____. (v. 1)

Truths about God:

d. **Psalm 18:1-3**, spoken by _____ on the day _____

_____(See the title given before v. 1)

Truths about God:

e. Psalm 31:2-5, a psalm of David during times of _____

_____ (Summarize from vv. 9-14)

Truths about God:

f. **Psalm 62:1-2, 5-8,** written by _____ as he waited for God. (v. 1)

When a believer recognizes God as his Rock, what will he do or not do?

g. Psalm 144:1-4, composed by David.

Truths about God:

2. British pastor Alexander MacLaren said:

"God is a rock for a foundation.
Build your lives, your thoughts, your efforts, your hopes there...

God is a rock for a fortress. Flee to Him to hide...

God is a rock for shade and refreshment.
Come close to Him from out of the scorching heat,
and you will find coolness and verdure [things green and growing]
and moisture in the clefts when all outside that grateful shadow is parched and dry."[5]

Also, consider that a large rock is:

solid, stable, permanent, unchanging, protective, strong and sheltering.

Which of the characteristics of a rock, stated in either the quote or list above, would provide the most comfort and hope in times of depression? Circle all that would be of help, and then record the one you feel is most important to you in the box below.

3. It is interesting to note that one of the ways believers think of God as they near the end of life on earth is as a rock. Just before his death, Moses composed a song where he refers to God as "the Rock" (Deuteronomy 32:4). Similarly, toward the end of his own tumultuous life, David composed a song to the LORD that begins, "The LORD is my rock..." (2 Samuel 22:2, see also 23:3); and in the end times, Israel will sing a song that says:

> *"Trust in the LORD forever,*
> *For in YAH, the LORD, is **everlasting strength**."*
> Isaiah 26:4

a. In this verse, the words translated "everlasting strength" are literally "a Rock of Ages." Read this verse out loud, inserting the literal meaning.

b. Using all you have learned, record your thoughts as you close out your study of God as your Rock.

4. God is our Rock—and obedience to His Word is the foundation we must lay for stability in life. One well-known hymn written by Fanny J. Crosby is entitled "He Hideth My Soul." Read (or sing!) some of the words of this wonderful song, and then end with the short prayer that follows.

> A wonderful Saviour is Jesus my Lord,
> A wonderful Saviour to me;
> He hideth my soul in the cleft of the rock,
> Where rivers of pleasure I see.
>
> He hideth my soul in the cleft of the rock
> That shadows a dry, thirsty land;
> He hideth my life in the depths of His love,
> And covers me there with His hand,
> And covers me there with His hand.
>
> A wonderful Saviour is Jesus my Lord,
> He taketh my burden away;
> He holdeth me up, and I shall not be moved,
> He giveth me strength as my day.[6]

LORD God, my Saviour,

Thank You for revealing Yourself as the eternal Rock of Ages. Help me to know you as my Rock, as Moses and David knew you. I want to look to You alone for strength, power and stability. Help me to see that You are my foundation rock and the cleft in which I can take refuge. Cause me to run to You and to Your Word when all around me is in turmoil. Throughout this life, remind me continually that you are my hiding place...and when my time on earth is coming to an end, may my song exalt the Rock that has been my everlasting strength!

Thoughts, Meditations and Prayers

*W*hy, LORD?

*I*n Psalm 119:71, the psalmist makes an astounding statement. He says:

"It is good for me that I have been afflicted..."

In Romans 8:28, the apostle Paul says:

"And we know that all things work together for good to those who love God,
to those who are the called according to His purpose."

How could it be good to be afflicted? What good could possibly come from some of life's worst trials? Again, Scripture has the answer.

Below are ten good things that God often brings out of the trials and sufferings of believers.

Read through all ten titles, and then choose *at least* four to study in more depth by reading the Scripture passages given *(read only bold passages if time is limited)* and then recording at least one of the following:

1) a portion of the bolded passage
2) a hymn that comes to mind, or
3) a time in your life when you have seen this good come out of a trial or suffering.

Some Reasons for Trials, Adversity and Suffering

1. TO PERFECT US—Psalm 66:10-12; **Romans 5:3-5**, 8:28-29; Hebrews 2:10

To make us more like Christ (conform us to the image of Christ). A silversmith knows when silver is pure by looking into it. He continues heating it and purifying it until he can look into it and see a perfect image of himself. "Perfect" (in the Greek) means complete or fully qualified.

2. TO PROVE US—1 Peter 1:7, 4:12-13; James 1:2-4; Psalm 26:2-3; **Job 23:10**

Perseverance in the faith is one evidence of genuine salvation. When we go through trials with our faith remaining strong, it proves to us and to others Who He is and Whose we are!

Remember: *For the four you choose to study, record 1) a portion of the bolded passage, 2) a hymn that comes to mind, or 3) a time in your life when you have seen this good come out of a trial or suffering.*

3. TO PREPARE US

    FOR WORK HERE—**Luke 22:31-32**, 2 Corinthians 1:4-7

      Each of us has a special place in strengthening the body of Christ.

    FOR REIGNING WITH HIM LATER—2 Timothy 2:12; **2 Thessalonians 1:4-5**

      Scripture teaches that suffering here will have future meaning.

4. TO PRESENT US WITH OPPORTUNITIES—**Acts 16:23-33**; Philippians 2:25-30

There are many examples in the Word where the LORD used times of adversity to spread the gospel.

5. TO PREVENT US FROM SINNING—**2 Corinthians 12:1-10**

Sometimes, God's purpose in adversity is to keep us from being sinfully self-confident or prideful.

6. TO PARENT US—**Hebrews 12:5-13**; Proverbs 3:11-12; Hosea 5:15-6:3; Psalm 119:67, 71

Other words here would be to "pressure" or "prod" us to walk in a manner worthy of the Lord Jesus Christ. As with any good parent, if a child will not respond to verbal instruction, the result is a parental "work" of one type or another that will cause the child to listen and obey. As our Father, God's instructions and works always flow from His heart of love.

7. TO PRUNE US AND PREPARE US FOR SPIRITUAL GROWTH—**John 15:1-2, 5, 8**

Suffering acts as spiritual "pruning." Without it there would not be full spiritual maturity nor abundant fruitfulness. Nothing that God permits is accidental or without design.

(Note the progression beginning in verse 1 from bearing "fruit," to verse 2 bearing "more fruit," to verses 5 and 8...)

8. TO PARTAKE OF HIS COMFORT, MERCY AND GRACE—**2 Corinthians 1:3-7**

Sometimes, God may let earthly comforts or comforters fail us so that, by turning to Him, we will experience a comfort and outpouring of mercy and grace that would never be known otherwise.

9. TO PROCLAIM HIS WORK AND LIFE—**John 9:1-3**; 2 Corinthians 4:7-15

Our ultimate purpose in life is to bring God glory, giving a correct estimate or opinion of who He is. Are you willing for your life to glorify Him in the way He sovereignly chooses?

10. TO PROFIT US ETERNALLY—**2 Corinthians 4:16-18**; Romans 5:2-5, 8:16-18; 2 Thessalonians 1:4-5; Hebrews 11:1, 10, 13-16, 27; James 1:2, 12;

We are called to live life with an eternal perspective, and that includes weighing each and every trial in light of the glory to come. It is only in doing this that we can begin to "count it all joy."

Summary:

In times of trial, many godly people have asked, "Why, LORD?" However, God does not usually choose to show us the exact reasons for our sufferings while we are in the midst of them. J. Sidlow Baxter explains one reason this is so:

> "...there are *some* things about human suffering which God cannot possibly explain to us without destroying the very purpose which they are designed to fulfill."[3]

In His Word, God has given us abundant promises to show us that He knows, hears and cares about our sufferings. And although they are not to be our focus, He has also graciously revealed many possible reasons for our trials.

End your time today in a prayer of thanksgiving to God for His Word and His works.

Thank Him that He is with you through all the trials of this life.
>   Thank Him for the promises in His Word and for the certain hope that, one day, your trials will end.
>   Thank Him that everything you experience will work for His glory and the good of all who love Him.

Then sing a favorite song of praise, and initial the box.

Thoughts, Meditations and Prayers

Hear my cry, O God;
Attend to my prayer.

From the end of the earth I will cry to You,
When my heart is overwhelmed;
Lead me to the rock that is higher than I.

For You have been a shelter for me,
A strong tower from the enemy.

I will abide in Your tabernacle forever;
I will trust in the shelter of Your wings.

Psalm 61:1-4

Lesson *Four*

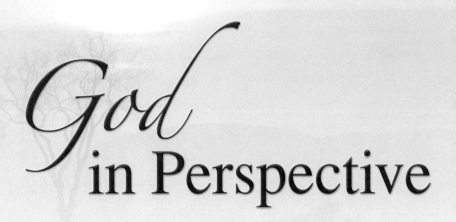

God in Perspective

"For as the heavens are higher than the earth,
So are My ways higher than your ways,
And My thoughts than your thoughts."

Isaiah 55:9

I'm not known for my love of flying. I will, however, admit to totally enjoying the part of a flight when the plane has leveled off, food has been served and I can look out over a vast carpet of clouds, watching the setting sun glisten and dance over them. It is an awe-inspiring sight that I can never see from below.

Although (thankfully) most of my flights have taken place on beautiful days with very little turbulence, on the morning of one flight, I awoke to thunder, lightening and torrential rain. How would my stomach survive the turbulence that was sure to accompany a stormy take-off? I can't read in the car without feeling sick (and I avoid even the "kiddie" roller coasters at theme parks)!

Though I do not think that being a little nervous about a flight is sinful, I was beginning to let my thoughts run wild into "What if..." territory. That was sin. 1 Corinthians 10:13 says, "No temptation has overtaken you except such as is common to man; but God is faithful, who will not allow you to be tempted beyond what you are able, but with the temptation will also make the way of escape, that you may be able to bear it." That is exactly what God provided: a way of escape.

What was it? No, God didn't have the airline cancel my flight, and He didn't end the storm. Instead, He gave me a new perspective. He brought to mind my previous flights where the plane had passed through the clouds to beautiful skies and bright sunlight. With those thoughts, my perspective changed. God was able see my plane through the storm to the beauty and peace that were already above it.

Perspective makes all the difference. Mount Everest towers high above hikers starting out to conquer it, yet when seen from the perspective of space, it is not nearly so large or magnificent. It's all a matter of perspective.

While physical perspective can calm, humble and inspire, spiritual perspective is even more powerful in our lives. The most important perspective we can have, spiritually speaking, is an accurate understanding of God: Who He is and what He is like. We cannot allow one or two of His attributes to obscure the whole picture of who He is.

Just as I had to remember that the sun was shining above the storm, we must remember *all* God's excellencies during the "storms" of life. We must not allow an inflated view of man to obscure His greatness, and we must not allow obstacles to appear bigger than God is. A complete and full perspective of God will be the most awe-inspiring sight our eyes (both physical and spiritual) will ever see!

Sovereign God,

You are greater than all my fears, problems and frailties.
May the time I spend in Your Word give me a greater understanding of
Your power, majesty and love.

PART ONE

> *Lead me to the rock that is higher than I.*
> For _____ *have been a shelter for me.*
> A _____ _____ *from the enemy."*
> Psalm 61:2b-3

$\mathcal{G}$od is love. He is also holy, merciful, faithful, kind, compassionate, just, righteous, and gracious.

Keep all of these attributes in mind as you study yet another of His attributes: His **sovereignty**, or in other words, **God's absolute rule, control, and supreme rank and power over all things**. If you focus *only* on His sovereignty, forgetting all His other characteristics, you may find the truths in this lesson hard to embrace. However, if you consider *all* His attributes, you will find that your God is infinitely more lovely than you can imagine!

The book of Job is familiar to many. You may recall that Job was a righteous man who, for reasons unknown to him, suffered much. The last chapters in this book record God's words as He brings Job (and us!) face to face with His sovereignty.

Oh, the wisdom of God! If someone asked us what one thing a suffering friend would most need to know about God, few of us would answer: "confront him with God's sovereignty." Yet this is what God did with Job—and with astounding benefit!

1. Who was Job? Briefly record what you learn from **Job 1:1-3** and 29:1-25.

2. What did Job suffer? Answer from:

a. **Job 1:13-19**

b. **Job 2:7-8**

c. **Job 2:9-10**

d. **Job 12:4a**, 17:6

3. Summarize the different ways in which Job responded to his suffering.

    a. *(Initial response)* **Job 1:20-22**

    b. **Job 3:1-3, 11**

    c. **Job 7:11, 10:1-2**

    e. **Job 19:25-27**

    f. Job 27:3-6

4. In the midst of his suffering, what did Job know about the sovereignty of God (about God's absolute rule and control over all things)? Sum up his general areas of understanding in the column provided.

Job Knew of God's Sovereignty Over...

    a. **Job 9:4-10**

    b. **Job 10:8-9**

    c. Job 12:13-15

    d. **Job 14:1-2, 5**

    e. Job 23:13-14

5. From your study, how would you rate Job's understanding of God's sovereignty?

non-existent   average   well-developed

_____

6. How would you rate your understanding of God's sovereignty? Did you grow up with this teaching? How important do you think it is to have a well-developed sense of God's sovereignty? Why?

PART TWO

> *Lead me to the rock that is _____ than I.*
> *For You have been a _____ for _____ ,*
> *A _____ tower from the _____."*
> Psalm 61:2b-3

"The fairest face on earth, with the most comely features, would soon become ugly and unsightly, if one member continued growing while the others remained undeveloped."[1]

God's sovereignty is the focus again today, but do not forget all His other attributes. There is much beauty and comfort in having a sovereign God who is also completely just, wise, good, loving, faithful, kind, holy, merciful and righteous!

1. In Job 38, God begins a response to the suffering Job.

> *"Then the LORD answered Job out of the whirlwind, and said:*
> *'Who is this who darkens counsel by words without knowledge?*
> *Now prepare yourself like a man; I will question you, and you shall answer Me.'"*
> Job 38:1-3

a. In the passage above:
   1) Put boxes around God's commands to Job.
   2) Underline what God says He is going to do with Job.

b. Why might God begin responding to His suffering child with commands and questions? *(Review Job's statements in Job 13:3, 23:1-7 and 31:35-37 before you answer.)*

c. For three chapters (38-40), God stops Job's questions to ask His own questions. Some excerpts are written below. As you read, put a question mark on or over the one word that begins each of God's questions to Job (for example, put a question mark for each "who," "what," "where," "when," "how," "have," "can," etc.) and complete the boxes.

"Where were you when I laid the foundations of the earth? Tell Me, if you have understanding.

Who determined its measurements? Surely you know!

Or who stretched the line upon it?

To what were its foundations fastened?

Or who laid its cornerstone, when the morning stars sang together,

And all the sons of God shouted for joy?

Have you commanded the morning since your days began,

And caused the dawn to know its place...

> In your own words, summarize God's questions to Job thus far:

Have you entered the springs of the sea? Or have you walked in search of the depths?

Have you comprehended the breadth of the earth? Tell Me, if you know all this.

Where is the way to the dwelling of light?

And darkness, where is its place, that you may take it to its territory,

That you may know the paths to its home?

Do you know it, because you were born then, or because the number of your days is great?

Do you know the ordinances of the heavens?

Can you set their dominion over the earth?

Can you lift up your voice to the clouds, that an abundance of water may cover you?

Can you send out lightnings, that they may go, and say to you, 'Here we are!'?

Have you given the horse strength?

Have you clothed his neck with thunder?

Can you frighten him like a locust?

Does the hawk fly by your wisdom, and spread its wings toward the south?

Does the eagle mount up at your command, and make its nest on high?"

Job 38:4-7, 12, 16, 18, 19-21, 33-35 and 39:19-20a, 26-27

> What might God want Job to understand or recognize through these questions?

2. At the end of God's address, Job says some fascinating words in chapter 42:

> [1]*"Then Job answered the LORD and said,*
> [2]*'I know that You can do everything, and that no purpose of Yours can be withheld from You.*
> [3]*You asked, "Who is this who hides counsel without knowledge?"*
> *Therefore I have uttered what I did not understand, things too wonderful for me, which I did not know."*
>
> [5]*'I have heard of You by the hearing of the ear, But now my eye sees You.*
> [6]*Therefore I abhor myself, and repent in dust and ashes.'"*

a. Underline what Job says in verses five and six in the passage above.

b. In Part One, you saw that Job was already a godly and righteous man who feared the LORD and had a fairly good understanding of God's sovereignty. Why might he have said the words in verses 5-6?

c. Of what things might Job need to repent? Explain why you answer as you do.

d. Did Job's response of faith and repentance come before or after God lifted his suffering and restored his losses? Does it matter? Why or why not?

3. Among the many attributes God could have revealed to Job (His love, care, faithfulness, mercy, etc.), He chose to show His suffering child His sovereignty and transcendence (that He is greater than man). However, do you see *any* of God's love, care, faithfulness or mercy in His response to Job? If so, how?

4. Like Job, have you seen the glory, power, majesty and sovereignty of God today in a way you had not grasped it before? Do you have any heart attitudes or faithless actions that require repentance? If so, will you go now to the LORD for forgiveness?

5. If you are not familiar with the end of Job's story, take a few minutes to read the rest of Job 42.

PART THREE

"When I consider Your heavens, the work of Your fingers,
The moon and the stars, which You have ordained,
What is man that You are mindful of him...?"

Psalm 8:3-4a

Understanding God's sovereign rule and power causes us to put ourselves in a right perspective. He is God; we are human. He is infinite; we are finite. He knows all things; we see only in part. He is LORD; we are His.

Job had to take his eyes off of himself and his circumstances and put them on God. We can only have a right perspective of life when we have a right perspective of God. All too often, however, our focus is self-centered rather than God-centered. One of the best ways to take our eyes off self is to read the psalms, for they exalt God and put man in his proper place.

1. Psalm 145 is a magnificent psalm on the goodness, greatness, majesty and love of God. As you read it, make notes in the space provided below, focusing primarily on who God is and how He reveals Himself.

A Psalm for Perspective

Psalm 145

God's Character and Attributes	God's Promised Provisions	My Response

2. (*Optional*) Choose one or more of the following psalms to study in order to increase a God-centered perspective. On a separate sheet of paper, record the same headings as in the previous question. A short "title" of each psalm is given to help you choose which to study. (Shorter passages are in boldface type.)

Psalm 56   **A psalm for times of fear and danger**

Psalm 61   **On assurance of God's presence and protection** (*Your memory verse passage!*)

Psalm 68   On the glory of God

Psalm 71   A psalm for old age

Psalm 102   A prayer when in affliction

Psalm 104   On the sovereignty of God

Psalm 113   **On the majesty of God**

Psalm 139   Assurance God knows, cares and provides

3. End with a time of prayer, acknowledging God's sovereign rule over all things, committing to persevere in any trials He chooses to bring your way, and thanking Him for the comfort and blessings He promises those who patiently endure
        OR...
if you find the truth of God's sovereignty hard to accept, ask Him to help you come to the place where you love this teaching.

Thought for meditation:

God promises to provide a way of escape so that we are able to bear every circumstance He causes or allows. What "escape" did God provide for His suffering servant Job (before He relieved his suffering)?

Could it simply have been to show him Himself? Read 2 Corinthians 12:9.

Thoughts, Meditations and Prayers

Father of Mercies God of All Comfort

The dual name, "Father of mercies and God of all comfort," is located in Second Corinthians 1:3-4a, which says:

> *"Blessed be the God and Father of our Lord Jesus Christ,*
> *the Father of mercies and God of all comfort,*
> *who comforts us in all our tribulation..."*

James 5:11 says:

> *"Indeed we count them blessed who endure.*
> *You have heard of the perseverance of Job and seen the end intended by the Lord—*
> *that the Lord is very compassionate and merciful."*

One of the outcomes of Job's suffering was his knowing the LORD's great compassion and mercy. Indeed, this is a theme emphasized throughout all of Scripture.

What would God have you learn about His mercies and comfort today?

Section One: Father of Mercies

1. Psalm 103 praises God for His mercies. As you read it, record all you learn about the mercy of the LORD, whether by direct statements or by the things He does. Also, record principles, ideas or examples that will help you respond rightly to God's mercy. Be as thorough as time allows—there are many blessings in these wonderful verses! There is additional space on the following page, so write all you can!

Psalm 103
Truths About God's Mercies

In light of God's mercies:
My Responses

2. In this psalm, particularly note the terms used to describe God's mercy in:

v. 4

v. 8

v. 11

v. 17

3. Proverbs 3:3 says:

"Let not mercy and truth forsake you;
Bind them around your neck, write them on the tablet of your heart"

Regarding this verse, Pastor John MacArthur says,
"The virtues of mercy...and truth that come from God are to become part of us—outwardly in our behavior for all to see as an adornment of spiritual beauty, and inwardly as the subject of our meditation."[7]

Review your entries on the list in question one. Are the truths of God's mercy engraved on your heart? Have you studied them enough for them to be written there permanently?

If you said "no, but I wish they were," will you spend some time now meditating on the mercies of God and asking Him to make His mercies real to your heart?

If you said "yes," do others consistently see and hear of God's mercies through you?

94

Section Two: *God of All Comfort*

$\mathcal{N}$ot only is God the Father (originator) of mercy, He is also the God of **all** comfort. However, as you will see, this does not simply mean that God always makes us "comfortable," "at ease," and without discomfort.

God uses many word pictures in Scripture to help us understand spiritual realities. Many of these illustrations bring immeasurable comfort to the heart while helping us understand the nature of the comfort that God provides.

1. Below are some of the "comforting" word pictures found in Scripture.

> Look up the initial verse, recording the appropriate word in each blank.
> Write out one phrase or portion of the verse that contains the word picture.
> Answer any questions that follow.

α. **2 Corinthians 6:18**   God is described as a _____.

Portion of the verse containing the word picture:

> Read these additional verses that refer to God as a Father. Note significant words, phrases, actions or thoughts that relate to God as a Father.

1) **2 Samuel 7:14-15a** *(see also Hebrews 12:5-11)*

"I will be his Father, and he shall be My son.
If he commits iniquity, I will chasten him...
But my mercy shall not depart from him..."

2) **Psalm 103:13**

"As a father pities his children, so the LORD pities
those who fear Him. For He knows our frame;
He remembers that we are dust."

3) Romans 8:14-17

"For as many as are led by the Spirit of God,
these are sons of God...you received the Spirit
of adoption by whom we cry out, 'Abba, Father.'"

What thoughts do you have regarding the comfort of having a God who is also your Father?

b. **Psalm 91:4**   God is described as having _____.

Portion of the verse containing the word picture:

1) In his commentary on Deuteronomy, John MacArthur says, "The Lord exercised His loving care for Israel like an eagle caring for its young, especially as they were taught to fly. As they began to fly and had little strength, they would start to fall. At that point, an eagle would stop their fall by spreading its wings so they could land on them; so the Lord has carried Israel and not let the nation fall. He has been training Israel to fly on His wings of love and omnipotence."[8]

With this thought in mind, read and note the descriptive phrases in the following passages.

a) **Deuteronomy 32:11-12a**

"As an eagle stirs up its nest, hovers over its young,
spreading out its wings, taking them up,
carrying them on its wings, So the LORD..."

b) **Deuteronomy 33:26-27**

"There is no one like the God of Jeshurun,
Who rides the heavens to help you,
and in His excellency on the clouds.
The eternal God is your refuge,
And underneath are the everlasting arms"

c) Exodus 19:4

"You have seen what I did to the Egyptians, and how I bore
you on eagles' wings and brought you to Myself."

d) Psalm 57:1, 63:7

"...in the shadow of Your wings I will make my refuge,
Until these calamities have passed by."

"Because You have been my help,
Therefore in the shadow of Your wings I will rejoice."

In what way might this word picture bring comfort and hope to someone experiencing feelings of depression or anxiety?

---

c. **Psalm 90:1** God is described as a _____ _____.

Portion of the verse containing the word picture:

1) **Acts 17:28** *(see also John 17:20-21)*

"for in Him we live and move and have our being..."

<blockquote>
What comforts are there in having the LORD as your "dwelling place?" Spend a few moments pondering this picture before you answer.
</blockquote>

2. Of the word pictures you have studied, which one brings the most comfort to your heart? Why?

3. How do believers receive the comfort of God today? Record what you learn from:
a. John 14:16-18

b. Romans 15:4 *(if you have time, also see also Psalm 119:49-50)*

c. 2 Corinthians 1:4 *(see also 1 Peter 3:8)*

4. Often without even realizing what we are doing, the tendency in times of depression is to cut ourselves off from one or more of these God-given sources of comfort. What are some ways in which we might do this?

5. Although written to the nation of Israel, Isaiah 51 contains principles of comfort for God's people today. Read the following excerpts out loud:

"'Listen to Me, you who follow after righteousness, You who seek the LORD' ...

For the LORD will comfort Zion, He will comfort all her waste places;
He will make her wilderness like Eden,
And her desert like the garden of the LORD;
Joy and gladness will be found in it, thanksgiving and the voice of melody...

'I, even I, am He who comforts you.
Who are you that you should be afraid of a man who will die,
And of the son of a man who will be made like grass?
And you forget the LORD your Maker, Who stretched out the heavens and laid the foundations of the earth...

But I am the LORD your God, Who divided the sea whose waves roared—
The LORD of hosts is His name. And I have put My words in your mouth;
I have covered you with the shadow of My hand...
You are My people.'"

Circle some of the phrases above that you would like to use in a prayer of thanksgiving to your God. Then pray, thanking Him that He is the Father of mercies and the God of all comfort. Ask Him to be as a Father to you, giving you what you need, but not necessarily what you want. When you are done, initial the box.

A Sacrifice of Praise

*"Therefore by Him let us continually offer the sacrifice of praise to God,
that is, the fruit of our lips, giving thanks to His name."*

Hebrews 13:15

Sometimes, praise is the overflow of a heart that is rejoicing. Other times, the offering of praise to the LORD is a sacrifice of immense proportions. In times when the heart is sorrowful, defeated, fearful, lonely, unsure, or down, the attitude of praise to God is an act of sacrifice and obedience.

Every Christian desires to praise God; however, times of depression can make praising (or praying in general) difficult. If you take time to study the writings of the psalmists, you will find that in times of deep distress, they prayed prayers known as "laments." In these laments, they voiced their problems to God and made their petitions to Him. Many of their laments ended with praise. For example, notice the change to praise in verses five and six in the lament below:

1 *"How long, O LORD? Will You forget me forever?
How long will You hide Your face from me?*

2 *How long shall I take counsel in my soul, having sorrow in my heart daily?
How long will my enemy be exalted over me?*

3 *Consider and hear me, O LORD my God;
Enlighten my eyes, lest I sleep the sleep of death;*

4 *Lest my enemy say, 'I have prevailed against him';
Lest those who trouble me rejoice when I am moved.*

5 ***But*** *I have trusted in Your mercy;
My heart shall rejoice in Your salvation.*

6 *I will sing to the LORD,
Because He has dealt bountifully with me."*

Psalm 13

Today, learn from the praises of the psalmists. Some of their praises come from the beginning of the psalm (from an already rejoicing heart) and others from the end (often from a heart which has turned from lament to praise). Whether your heart is rejoicing or sorrowful, this lesson will help you put your hope in God as the Scriptures lead you into praise!

1. As you read the following praises, make notes under the appropriate columns on the chart provided.

I Will Praise

Names of God used in praise	Characteristics/Actions for which God is praised	Ways to Express praise to God
Psalm		
9:1-2		
18:1-3		
28:6-7		
30:1-5		
33:1-9, 20-22		
47:1-9		

2. Star two or three thoughts which stood out the most to you as you studied the words of praise and then record any additional observations about praise in the space below.

3. Did you notice how often the idea of music was mentioned? Do you regularly incorporate singing into your day? (This includes *listening* to songs of praise and adoration, but should not be limited to it!) If so, what is your favorite hymn or song of praise? If not, why might it be important, as a scriptural principle, to do so?

4. Now, pray back (or sing back!) Scripture to the LORD. Use His names in prayer, and make some of the words you recorded on your chart your own as you pray them back to God from your heart. If your heart is heavy, you may begin with a lament to the LORD, but be sure to end with praise! ☐

Hear my cry, O God;
Attend to my prayer.

From the end of the earth I will cry to You,
When my heart is overwhelmed;
Lead me to the rock that is higher than I.

For You have been a shelter for me,
A strong tower from the enemy.

I will abide in Your tabernacle forever;
I will trust in the shelter of Your wings.

Psalm 61:1-4

Lesson Five

What Do You Know?

"You are My flock, the flock of My pasture; you are men, and I am your God..."
Ezekiel 34:31

*O*nce again, my imagination was running wild. While my two small children were asleep in their beds and my military husband was deployed halfway around the world, I laid in bed thinking that every sound was an intruder. It was a huge struggle just to make myself stay put. I analyzed each noise: "It's just the creaking of the house...just the wind...just the ice-maker."

My thoughts began to stray further and further. "What if my husband never comes home? What if his plane crashes? What if I have to raise two children alone? What if I never see him again?"
I tried praying. "Lord, please keep us safe...please keep him safe." It seemed as if I was praying constantly. Yet hour followed hour, and I could not make myself sleep.

Finally, (I have now learned to do this first!) I turned my mind to what I had been learning in a Bible study on the names of God. In Psalm 23, God reveals that He is Jehovah-Raah, The LORD my Shepherd. I began to recall and meditate on the verses I had studied. I also recalled some thoughts from Phillip Keller's book *A Shepherd Looks at Psalm 23*, which I had been reading. He writes:

> "In the Christian's life there is no substitute for the keen awareness that my
> Shepherd is nearby. There is nothing like Christ's presence to dispel the fear,
> the panic, the terror of the unknown.

> "Generally it is the 'unknown,' the 'unexpected,' that produces the greatest
> panic. It is in the grip of fear that most of us are unable to cope with the cruel
> circumstances and harsh complexities of life. We feel they are foes which

endanger our tranquility. Often our first impulse is simply to get up and run from them.

"Then in the midst of our misfortunes there suddenly comes the awareness that He, the Christ, the Good Shepherd is there. It makes all the difference."[1]

As I completely occupied my mind with the knowledge that my Shepherd who never slumbers or sleeps (Psalm 121) was keeping watch over me, peaceful sleep followed close behind.

"I will both lie down in peace, and sleep;
For You alone, O LORD, make me dwell in safety."

Psalm 4:8

My LORD and God,

Thank You that You are the Shepherd of Your people.
Lead me, guide me and give me peace as I come to Your Word.

PART ONE

> For You have been a _____ for me.
> A strong tower from the enemy.
> I will _____ in Your tabernacle _____."
>
> Psalm 61:3-4

The book of Habakkuk has had a tremendous impact on people through all ages, for in it a believer (Habakkuk) comes to see one of the most necessary truths for life on earth: "The just shall live by faith."

1. During the time of Habakkuk, the people of the LORD were in a state of ongoing sin, straying from God. This prophet prays to God, asking how long the LORD will wait before bringing judgment and disciplining His children.

Read Habakkuk 1:2-3.

2. God responds by telling Habakkuk that He is not indifferent and that judgment is coming. In fact, God tells Habakkuk that he won't even be able to understand or believe His plans.

Read Habakkuk 1:5

3. God's judgment will be to raise up the ruthless, deadly and self-promoting Chaldeans (Babylonians) as discipline for His own people.

Read Habakkuk 1:6-10

4. As God had said, Habakkuk does have a hard time believing his ears! The LORD's plan makes no sense to him. He knows that the LORD is holy; yet God says that He will use an evil, pagan nation to conquer and bring judgment upon His own people. Note the extensive use of the names of God as Habakkuk begins his objections to God's plan in verses 12-13. (Underline each name as you see it.)

> "Are You not from everlasting,
> O LORD my God, my Holy One? We shall not die.
> O LORD, You have appointed them for judgment;
> O Rock, You have marked them for correction.
> You are of purer eyes than to behold evil, and cannot look on wickedness.
> Why do You look on those who deal treacherously,
> And hold Your tongue when the wicked devours a person more righteous than he?

a. How many names of God did Habakkuk use?

b. *(Optional)* Remembering that God's names reveal His nature and character, why do you think Habakkuk uses God's names so much in his objection to God's plan?

5. Habakkuk then shows total trust in God and God's plan when he determines to wait patiently and expectantly for the LORD's answer.

Read Habakkuk 2:1

6. God responds, telling Habakkuk that a good end will surely come—but not immediately. Although Habakkuk must be patient, he can know that the end will not be late.

Read Habakkuk 2:2-3

7. God then contrasts the pagan nation with those who know the LORD (2:4). The last phrase of Habakkuk 2:4 summarizes how believers are to live. Write it below.

8. Habakkuk responds with a song stating his commitment to wait on the LORD with faith, even through bad times that are sure to come at the hands of the conquering Chaldeans. He would not live by what he could see. Instead, he would live by faith in God's Word and character.

   a. List the circumstances in which Habakkuk anticipates the need to live by faith. (Habakkuk 3:17)

   b. How would Habakkuk respond to these hard circumstances which would certainly accompany the coming invasion? (Habakkuk 3:18)

   c. How does Habakkuk end his psalm of faith? (v. 19)

9. Hebrews 11:1 gives a biblical definition of faith:

    "Now faith is the substance of things hoped for, the evidence of things not seen."

   a. Using your own words, what does it mean to "live by faith"?

10. What are some modern day "no bloom, no fruit" occurrences that call for believers to live by faith as they wait to see the promises of the LORD? Add more entries to the list below.

Today we must live by faith during times of...

> *Illness*
> *Unemployment*
> *Terror threats*

11. Like Habakkuk, do you know the promises of God regarding help, deliverance and ultimate victory? If so, write at least two of His precious promises below. If not, take time now to read some of God's promises in Appendix C, and write one in the space below.

12. Are you living by faith as you wait for the fulfillment of the LORD's promises to you? Like Habakkuk, are you committed to waiting even when "the fig tree does not bloom?" (Habakkuk 3:17) If so, let the LORD know your heart as you close this part of study with prayer.

PART TWO

> *For You have been a shelter for me.*
> *A _____ tower from the enemy.*
> *I _____ abide in _____ _____ forever."*
> Psalm 61:3-4

*T*he way I usually describe "living by faith" is:

LIVE BY WHAT YOU KNOW, NOT BY WHAT YOU FEEL.

I have said these words to myself so many times, and for so long, that I do not know if I heard them somewhere or if they are original with me. I just know that these are words that I must remind myself of every day...because feelings can be overpowering and deceptive. Feelings are a wonderful gift from God, but I must let true, godly thoughts control how I feel, and not allow how I feel to control my thoughts.

Let me tell you an illustration I heard once. When viewing a scary movie, your heart often begins to beat a little faster and you begin to feel anxiety and even some fear. There is no real reason for this, as you know it is only a movie. However, for the moment, the plot of the movie controls your thoughts and your body reacts with anxious feelings.

The same thing happens in a sad movie. Even though you know that the actor is not really dying, your feelings are controlled by the things you are thinking about, and you may begin to cry.

That's the point...feelings respond to thoughts with little concern for what is real or true. This is why verse after verse in Scripture says to control what goes into the mind and what we allow ourselves to think about. This is the only way to live a life that is pleasing to God and pleasant for us and others...it is the only way to live a holy, self-controlled and stable life.

1. **It is interesting to note that the Bible never commands us to change our feelings. Rather, our feelings will change as we control our thoughts in obedience to God's Word.**

 a. Fill in the blanks in the passages below.

"'You shall love the LORD your God with all your heart,
with all your soul,

and _____ _____ _____ _____ *.'*
This is the first and great commandment."
Matthew 22:37

"Finally, brethren, whatever things are true,
whatever things are noble,
whatever things are just,
whatever things are pure,
whatever things are lovely,
whatever things are of good report,
if there is any virtue and if there is anything praiseworthy—

[Let your mind] _____ _____ _____ _____ *."*
Philippians 4:8

 b. Read again the bold sentences above. Write the main thoughts out below (using your own words if you wish).

2. Through Scripture, the Almighty God of the Universe speaks directly to you. Are you prepared to believe what He says, regardless of what your feelings tell you? Will you love Him "with all your mind"? If so, initial the box. If not, why not?

3. Read the following verses and answer the questions which follow each one. When possible, use the exact words of Scripture in your answer.

   a. 1 Corinthians 10:13

> *"No temptation has overtaken you except such as is common to man;*
> *but God is faithful, who will not allow you to be tempted beyond what you are able,*
> *but with the temptation will also make the way of escape, that you may be able to bear it."*

   1) According to this verse, are you the only one who has ever experienced your particular troubles?
      Note: "common to man" literally means "that which is human"

      Check any of the following areas in which problems have affected your life:

physical	hurts from your past	fear of possible calamities
financial	lost chances	weight problems
marriage	past mistakes	failures
child-rearing	feelings	depression
childlessness	lack of feelings	loneliness
extended family	career/school	_____

      (fill in your own)

      (All people would check several items in the list above.
      These are all simply a part of being human in a fallen, sinful world.
      These are some of the "all things" God will work together for our good.
      The way we respond in the midst of these trials is what makes all the difference.)

   2) What do you learn about God from this passage?

      What He is: _____.

      What He will not allow:_____

      What He will make:_____
      *[Note: the escape is **never** self-murder (suicide), for He has said, "Thou shalt not murder." (Exodus 20:13)]*

      Why He will do this:_____

   3) Choose one of the following sentences to sum up the truths of this passage. Write it on the line below.

      God promises the ability to overcome sin in any temptation or trial.
      My suffering is not unique. It is part of being human.
      My suffering will never be too much to bear.

      _____

   4) Check one of the following statements:

      ☐ I believe and feel this to be true
      ☐ I choose to believe this, but do not feel it at the moment
      ☐ I do not believe this

      [Note: Whether or not you believe this does not affect its truth. God's Word IS truth.
      However, your belief in His truth does affect your life.]

b. James 1:2-6

> [2]*"My brethren, count it all joy when you fall into various trials,* [3]*knowing that the testing of your faith produces patience.* [4]*But let patience have its perfect work, that you may be perfect and complete, lacking nothing.* [5]*If any of you lacks wisdom, let him ask of God, who gives to all liberally and without reproach, and it will be given him.* [6]*But let him ask in faith, with no doubting, for he who doubts is like a wave of the sea driven and tossed by the wind."*

1) When we face trials or adversity, how are we to think about them (consider them)? (v.2)

2) What is another term used for "trial" in verse 3?

   testing _____ _____ _____

3) What does this testing of your faith produce or develop? (v. 3)
   (This is one of the reasons we can consider it all joy!)

4) According to verse 4, what will be the final result of trials you encounter?

   [Note: "perfect" (NKJV and NAS) does not mean "sinless." Rather, it has the idea of spiritual maturity.]

5) According to verse 6, how are you to ask God for wisdom?

   (Note: "without doubting" refers to having a mind that is not divided by indecision or distrust.)

6) When we ask God for wisdom in dealing with our trials, how does He give it? (v. 5)

7) In one sentence, sum up the truths in this passage.
   (You may use the example below or write your own.)

   As a believer, my trials will result in my growth in spiritual maturity and stability.

   _____

   _____

8) Check one of the following statements:
   ☐ I believe and feel this to be true
   ☐ I choose to believe this, but do not feel it at the moment
   ☐ I do not believe this

4. Review your answers from today's study. Which truth do you most need to keep in mind?

PART THREE

> For _____ _____ _____ *a shelter for* _____ .
>
> *A strong tower* _____ _____ _____ .
>
> _____ _____ _____ *in Your tabernacle forever."*
>
> Psalm 61:3-4

*H*aving an increasing knowledge of God's Word is essential to thinking correctly and biblically about your circumstances. If you are a believer, God, through the power of the Holy Spirit, will use His Word to change your life by transforming your thoughts. As He transforms your thoughts, your feelings will come in line with reality.

1. God says over and over to guard your mind and your thoughts. In the following verses,

   1. Mark a large "M" on top of the word "mind" when you see it.
   2. Beside each verse, write out what you are to do with your mind.
   3. Record the results of doing so (if stated).

a. "...know the God of your father, and serve Him with a loyal heart and with a willing mind;"
1 Chronicles 28:9

a. To Do _____
_____

b. "You will keep him in perfect peace, Whose mind is stayed on You, because he trusts in You."
Isaiah 26:3

b. To Do _____
Result _____

c. "Yet this I call to mind, And therefore I have hope: Because of the LORD's great love we are not consumed, For His compassions never fail. They are new every morning; great is Your faithfulness."
Lamentations 3:21-23 (NIV)

c. To Do _____
Result _____
_____

d. "Let this mind be in you which was also in Christ Jesus, who...made Himself of no reputation, taking the form of a bondservant... He humbled Himself and became obedient to the point of death." Philippians 2:5-8

d. To Do _____
_____

e. "Therefore gird up the loins of your mind, be sober, and rest your hope fully upon the grace that is to be brought to you at the revelation of Jesus Christ;"
1 Peter 1:13

e. To Do _____
_____

[NOTE: "gird up the loins" carries the idea of gathering together loose pieces]

f. "And do not be conformed to this world, but be transformed by the renewing of your mind, that you may prove what is that good and acceptable and perfect will of God."
Romans 12:2

f. To Do _____
_____
Result _____

111

2. Thoughts are so fickle when left to themselves! They will run from one thing to another, telling you whatever your flesh wants to hear. And when they do so, they inevitably produce feelings that are hard to control.

When you find your thoughts running wild and untamed, you must come against those thoughts and force them out.

> *"...casting down arguments and every high thing*
> *that exalts itself against the knowledge of God,*
> *bringing every thought into captivity to the obedience of Christ."*
> 2 Corinthians 10:5

When you determine that a thought is contrary to the Word of God, put it out and **tell yourself truth about God** instead. Repeat truth to yourself over and over until the thought has completely left. If it returns, put it out again, and tell yourself the truth all over again. This will take a lot of time and effort at first, but it will get easier with practice and perseverance!

To do this, it is usually most effective to **talk out loud**. Thinking it *and* hearing it seem to dispel the unbiblical thoughts more quickly.

The more of God's Word you **memorize**, the more effective this will be. You will have at hand the weapon you need: the sword of the Spirit, which is the Word of God (Ephesians 6:17). Writing down verses on cards and posting them or keeping them readily available will also help.

Every day brings temptation to think unbiblical thoughts which can cause feelings capable of hindering a Christian's life and walk. The next two pages contain several unbiblical thoughts that can gain a foothold in the mind and cause or deepen feelings of depression.

As you read each entry on the following two pages:

a. Put a check mark below any thoughts in the first column that have been (or remain) a problem in your life.

b. Read the biblical truth in the second column.

c. Read the first verse, which is already written out in the third column.

d. Write out the second verse under its reference, again in the third column.

THOUGHTS WHICH DEEPEN DEPRESSION	TRUTH TO KNOW	HOW TO KNOW IT
Nobody understands what I'm going through.	God understands everything and has great power to help.	**Hebrews 4:14-16** *"...we have a great High Priest who has passed through the heavens, Jesus the Son of God, let us hold fast our confession. For we do not have a High Priest who cannot sympathize with our weaknesses, but was in all points tempted as we are, yet without sin. Let us therefore come boldly to the throne of grace, that we may obtain mercy and find grace to help in time of need."* **Psalm 147:5** _____
Nobody has gone through what I am having to go through.	My suffering is nothing new or unusual. Many have suffered as much or more.	**Hebrews 11:36-37** *"Still others had trial of mockings and scourgings, yes, and of chains and imprisonment. They were stoned, they were sawn in two, were tempted, were slain with the sword. They wandered about in sheepskins and goatskins, being destitute, afflicted, tormented..."* **1 Corinthians 10:13a**
If I try again, I'll probably just fail again.	With His help and power, I can do all the things Christ commands me to do ...I need not fear.	**2 Timothy 1:7** *"For God has not given us a spirit of fear, but of power and of love and of a sound mind."* **Philippians 2:13**
Maybe others can make it, but I can't.	I have been given all I need to live an abundant life that pleases the Lord.	**2 Peter 1:3** *"...His divine power has given to us all things that pertain to life and godliness..."* _____ **Philippians 4:13**

THOUGHTS WHICH DEEPEN DEPRESSION	TRUTH TO KNOW	
I'm a failure...and everyone knows it.	Everyone has failed in some area...what matters is not what anyone thinks, but that I keep on running the race.	**1 Timothy 6:12** *"Fight the good fight of faith, lay hold on eternal life, to which you were also called and have confessed the good confession in the presence of many witnesses."* **Philippians 3:12**
Things will never get better.	Trials are just for a while, and when they are done, if I have been obedient, I will be more like Christ.	**1 Peter 1:6** *"...though now for a little while, if need be, you have been grieved by various trials..."* **1 Peter 5:10**
God doesn't answer my prayers.	God hears and answers prayer, though not always as we think, and not always with a "yes."	**Isaiah 30:19b** *"...He will be very gracious to you at the sound of your cry; When he hears it, He will answer you."* **Psalm 138:3a**
I don't like myself.	God created me the way I am for His reasons and purposes. Therefore, I can praise Him. It is not for me to pass judgment on God's design, but to accept and praise His wisdom.	**Isaiah 64:8** *"But now, O LORD, You are our Father; We are the clay, and You our potter; And all we are the work of Your hand."* **Psalm 139:14**

Did you remember to place a check mark in the left-hand column below any thoughts that have been or remain a problem in your life?

3. It is important to remember the saying that began Part Two (the one that got me thinking and acting in obedience). It is:

LIVE BY WHAT YOU KNOW, NOT BY WHAT YOU FEEL.

Write this saying in the *"Thought for meditation"* box below, and then end with a time of prayer. Tell God that you commit to order your thoughts according to His Word and to live by faith with His help and power...and if you placed any check marks on the chart, include a time of repentance and confession!

Thought for meditation:

Spend a short time reviewing the memory verses you have learned to this point.

A Memory Verse Review for Psalm 61:

"Hear my cry, O _____ ;

Attend to my _____ .

From the _____ of the earth I will _____ to You,

When my _____ is overwhelmed;

Lead me to _____ _____ that is higher than I.

For _____ have been a _____ for me,

A _____ tower from the enemy.

I will _____ in Your tabernacle _____ ;

If you were unsure of any of the words above, look up the correct word(s) and fill in all the blanks; then read or recite the completed verses out loud...more than once, if time permits!

Thoughts, Meditations and Prayers

Jehovah-Raah The LORD my Shepherd

"He will feed His flock like a shepherd;
He will gather the lambs with His arm,
And carry them in His bosom,
And gently lead those who are with young."

Isaiah 40:11

God cares for and watches over His people. However, believers commonly doubt or forget this truth (whether evidenced by words or worry). Yet God's revelation of Himself as the Shepherd of His people illustrates His care for those who are His.

1. Although the LORD constantly and forever shepherds His people, there are times throughout life when His people are not as conscious of His presence as they are at other times. In fact, there are times when God does not seem to be a shepherd close at hand, protecting and providing—but a God far off and, dare we say, even unconcerned or unable to help.

The believer Job suffered more than most of us can imagine. In his great suffering and confusion, there was a time when Job could not sense the presence, care and protection of his God (his Shepherd).

"Look, I go forward, but He is not there,
And backward, but I cannot perceive Him;
When He works on the left hand, I cannot behold Him;
When He turns to the right hand, I cannot see Him."

Job 23:8-9

a. Underline the words or phrases that indicate Job does not sense God's presence.

b. Now record what Job continues on to say in Job 23:10-12. *(Be sure to notice the "But" that begins verse 10. He was not sensing God's presence, BUT...)*

2. When we experience difficult times, we must love the LORD our God with all our minds. We must remind ourselves over and over of the truths and promises of God's Word. We must live by faith: by what we cannot see, but know to be true. God's grace and His Word are sufficient for this.

What truths are essential to know (and live in light of!) about how God shepherds His people? Make notes on the following passages and then, with a goal of using six words or less, title or sum up each passage.

a. **Isaiah 40:11**

b. **John 10:11-13**

c. **John 10:14** (see also 10:2-4)

d. Hebrews 13:20-21

e. 1 Peter 2:25

f. **Revelation 7:16-17**

3. Psalm 23 is perhaps the most well-known of the psalms. It tells what believers can expect from the great Shepherd who leads, guides and works in them to do His will. Read the following verses out loud, whether for the first time or the hundredth!

¹ The LORD is my shepherd: I shall not want.

² He makes me to lie down in green pastures; He leads me beside the still waters.

³ He restores my soul; He leads me in the paths of righteousness for His name's sake.

⁴ Yea, though I walk through the valley of the shadow of death,
   I will fear no evil, for You are with me; Your rod and Your staff, they comfort me.

⁵ You prepare a table before me in the presence of my enemies;
   You anoint my head with oil; my cup runs over.

⁶ Surely goodness and mercy shall follow me all the days of my life;
   And I will dwell in the house of the LORD forever.

a. In the space below, record the phrase that expresses what you will not be in want of if the LORD is your Shepherd. The overall topic is given and a few are done for you.

v. 2   Rest   *He makes me to lie down*

v. 2   Guidance   *He leads me*

v. 2   Peace   *He leads me beside still (quiet) waters*

   v. 3   Restoration   _____

   v. 3   Guidance   _____

   v. 3   Righteousness _____

v. 4   Protection and courage   _____

v. 4   His presence,   _____

v. 4   Comfort   _____

   v. 5   Provision   *He prepares a table before me*

   v. 5   Protection   *He prepares a table before me in the presence of my enemies*

   v. 5   Blessings   _____

v. 6   Provision and His favor   _____

v. 6   A heavenly home   _____

v. 6   Security and relationship   _____

4. It is important to see that the psalmist David knew the LORD as his personal Shepherd.

Do you know Him as your Shepherd, also? Read through Psalm 23 again, this time putting your first initial over every occurrence of personal pronouns such as "my," "me," and "I."

5. What truth or passage from this study would you be most likely to share with someone?

6. The times when we can see or sense the leading and care of the LORD are wonderful; but when we cannot, then we must live by what we know. He is there and He is shepherding and caring for His own.

In her lovely devotional book about overcoming loss, June Titus says,

> "…I knew from past experience how hard it is to be glad in the midst of trials. That I did learn to be glad was because I looked, not to what I could see, but to the One I could believe. The power of God, my salvation by faith, and my heavenly inheritance were my hope and consolation. I could only walk by faith in God knowing that He promises to be with me and guide me."[9]

Will you begin or continue to follow the examples of Job, David, June Titus and so many others and walk by faith with your Shepherd?

Reflect on the following questions as you end your time of study, and then pray, thanking your God that He cares for you as a shepherd cares for His sheep and asking Him to make this truth real to you as you continue to meditate on His Word.

_____ Do you see yourself as a sheep and sense your need for a shepherd?

_____ Does your life give evidence that you are a sheep under the care of the good Shepherd?

_____ Do you listen for His voice and follow Him? In other words: Are you in the Word daily?

_____ Do you look to Him to provide for your every need...every day?
If you say "yes," how does your life give evidence of this?

As you end your time in prayer, ask God that you would never forget *all* His words imply when He says:

"You are my flock, the flock of My pasture; you are men, and I am your God..."

Ezekiel 34:31

Enemies of Hope

"'The LORD is my portion,' says my soul, 'Therefore I hope in Him!'"
Lamentations 3:24

As we recognize the LORD as our all-sufficient portion in life, we have hope.

In the midst of a tumultuous and sinful world, it is almost as if the LORD has set before us a table of provision that contains all we need for life, godliness, peace and perseverance. And as we explore the abundant provisions, we find that each and every one of them are ultimately God Himself.

As long as we do not allow things or circumstances to pull us away from seeing and living with God as our sufficiency and portion, hope need never waiver. Therefore, anything that takes our eyes off of God as our portion becomes the enemy of our hope.

Identifying these "enemies" is essential to strengthening our trust in the LORD as well as keeping and increasing our hope!

1. Answer the questions below, looking up verses as needed.

An Enemy of Hope	*Scripture*
a. <u>Unbelief</u>	*a.* *"Now may the God of hope fill you with all joy and peace <u>in believing</u>, that you may abound in hope by the power of the Holy Spirit."* Romans 15:13

This enemy has made its way into my life and thoughts: not at all   a little   too much   totally

Unbelief has affected my thoughts, attitudes and behavior in the following ways (if any):

We need not be overcome by unbelief when God is our portion. How does He help us combat this enemy? (*Use thoughts from* **Mark 9:24b**, *Philippians 1:29 and/or a verse of your choice.*)

b. _____

b. *"...I have learned in whatever state I am, to be <u>content</u>.* Philippians 4:11

"Now godliness with <u>contentment</u> is great gain." 1 Timothy 6:6

This enemy has made its way into my life and thoughts: not at all   a little   too much   totally

Discontentment has affected my thoughts, attitudes and behavior in the following ways (if any):

We need not be overcome by discontentment with God as our portion. How does He help us combat this enemy? *(Use thoughts from Ephesians 1:3-14, especially verse 3, and/or a verse of your choice.)*

_____

c. _____

c. *"Do all things without <u>grumbling</u> [murmuring] or <u>complaining</u> [negative questioning or criticizing]..."* Philippians 2:14

This enemy has made its way into my life and thoughts: not at all   a little   too much   totally

Grumbling and complaining have affected my thoughts, attitudes and behavior in the following ways (if any):

We will not be overcome by complaining when God is our portion. How does He help us combat this enemy? *(Use thoughts from 2 Corinthians 9:6-14, especially verse 8, and/or a verse of your choice.)*

_____

An Enemy of Hope   *Scripture*

d. <u>"If only" thoughts</u>

"If only my circumstances were different..."
"If only I had..."
"If only I hadn't..."
"If only someone else hadn't..."
"If only I could like myself..."

d. *"Finally, brethren, whatever things are* <u>*true*</u>*...meditate on these things."* Philippians 4:8

"...gird up the loins of your mind, be sober, and rest your hope fully on the grace that is to be brought to you at the revelation of Jesus Christ." 1 Peter 1:13

This enemy has made its way into my life and thoughts: not at all   a little   too much   totally

This enemy has affected my thoughts, attitudes and behavior in the following ways (if any):

We need not be overcome by "if only" thoughts when God is our portion. How does He help us combat this enemy? *(Use thoughts from Isaiah 26:3, **Isaiah 46:8-11**; Romans 8:28-30 and/or a verse of your choice.)*

---

e. <u>Comparing my own "lot in life" to others'</u>

e. *"When Peter saw him he asked; 'Lord, <u>what about this man?</u>' Jesus answered, 'If I want him to remain alive until I return, what is that to you? <u>You must follow Me</u>."* John 21:21-22

This enemy has made its way into my life and thoughts: not at all   a little   too much   totally

It has affected my thoughts, attitudes and behavior in the following ways (if any):

We need not be overcome by unbiblical comparisons when God is our portion. How does He help us combat this enemy? *(Use thoughts from Jeremiah 29:11 and/or a verse of your choice.)*

f. _____

f. "Therefore do not <u>worry about</u> tomorrow, for tomorrow will worry about itself. Each day has enough trouble of its own." Matthew 6:34 NIV

This enemy has made its way into my life and thoughts: not at all   a little   too much   totally

Worry has affected my thoughts, attitudes and behavior in the following ways (if any):

We need not be overcome by worry because God is our portion. How does He help us combat this enemy? *(Use thoughts from **Philippians 4:4-9**, Matthew 6:25-34 and/or a verse of your choice.)*

---

g. <u>Preoccupation with self:</u>
   a focus on "self" in any form including "self-esteem," "self-worth," or "self-hatred."

   We are all unworthy, we all fall short and we are all failures. Even so, every believer is accepted in Christ and now has His righteousness and worth imputed to us.

   The ultimate goal is for self to decrease and not be the focus at all.

g. "<u>I have been crucified</u> with Christ; it is no longer I who live..." Galatians 2:20

"He must increase, but <u>I must decrease</u>."
John 3:30

This enemy has made its way into my life and thoughts: not at all   a little   too much   totally

A preoccupation with self has affected my thoughts, attitudes and behavior in the following ways (if any):

We need not be overcome by preoccupation with self when God is our portion. How does He help us combat this enemy? *[Use thoughts from Galatians 2:20 and John 3:30 (written above), **2 Corinthians 4:7-11**, Colossians 3 and/or a verse of your choice.]*

An Enemy of Hope

h. <u>Dependence upon worldly wisdom</u>

Scripture

h. *"...that your faith should not be in the <u>wisdom</u> of men but in the power of God."*

1 Corinthians 2:5

This enemy has made its way into my life and thoughts: not at all   a little   too much   totally

I have been affected by the world's wisdom in the following ways (if any):

We need not be overcome by worldly wisdom because God is our portion. How does He help us combat this enemy? (*Use thoughts from **Colossians 2:3, Psalm 119:98-100,** James 1:5, 2 Peter 1:3-4 and/or a verse of your choice.*)

2. Of course, there are also other enemies that take our eyes off of God (and thus reduce our hope). For example, laying up treasures on earth instead of in heaven (Matthew 6:19-21) and seeing trials as "bad" instead of considering it all joy (James 1:2-4).

   a. Have either of these two enemies taken your thoughts off the LORD and His provision for your life? If so, which one?

   b. Can you think of other enemies that have taken your eyes off of God as your portion, satisfaction and hope?

   c. Which enemy of hope most often takes your eyes off the LORD as your portion?

   1) What is one practical and purposeful way you could combat this enemy and return your focus to the LORD?

3. Psalm 25 is about forgiveness and deliverance from enemies. Would you make the psalmist's words your prayer?

"To You, O LORD, I lift up my soul.
O my God, I trust in You;
Let me not be ashamed;
Let not my enemies triumph over me.
Indeed, let no one who waits on You be ashamed...

Show me Your ways, O LORD;
Teach me Your paths.
Lead me in Your truth and teach me,
For You are the God of my salvation;
On You I wait all the day.

Consider my enemies, for they are many;
And they hate me with cruel hatred.
Keep my soul, and deliver me;
Let me not be ashamed, for I put my trust in You.
Let integrity and uprightness preserve me,
For I wait for You."

Psalm 25:1-3a, 4-5, 19-21

Thoughts, Meditations and Prayers

Hear my cry, O God;
Attend to my prayer.

From the end of the earth I will cry to You,
When my heart is overwhelmed;
Lead me to the rock that is higher than I.

For You have been a shelter for me,
A strong tower from the enemy.

I will abide in Your tabernacle forever;
I will trust in the shelter of Your wings.

Psalm 61:1-4

Lesson Six

All Is Not Lost!

*"These things I have spoken to you, that in Me you may have peace.
In the world you will have tribulation; but be of good cheer,
I have overcome the world."*

John 16:33

"No known cure...not a lot is understood...research is ongoing..."

They say there are some things you can't really understand until you've experienced them. I found this to have some truth to it the day my son, Craig (then eleven years old), was diagnosed with Crohn's disease.* I could never have understood the cavernous hole that seemed to open in my heart when I heard the news of an illness without a cure. It was difficult to breathe, and no matter how hard I tried to be strong and not concern my son, I found it impossible to hold back some tears as the doctor's words went on and on.

During the hour-long drive home, Craig had questions for which his dad and I had no answers. However, one thing was clear: life as we had known it was gone forever. The future held medications, diet changes, side effects, hospitalizations, limitations on some physical activities and ever-present uncertainties.

We lost some things, that day. Craig lost a "normal" childhood, and we lost a "healthy" child. We grieved, and there were tears. However, we had not lost everything:

   We still had a loving God as our Heavenly Father (a Father who understands the heartache of seeing a son suffer!)

   We still had the comfort of knowing that this illness did not take our Father by surprise, and that He had everything under control.

---

*Crohn's disease is a condition in which the intestinal tract becomes inflamed. It can cause extreme pain and weight loss, among other things. Anti-inflammatory and immunosuppressant medications (such as steroids and chemotherapy) are often used to treat it.

We still had the promise that this trial would turn out for our good, our son's good, others' good and the glory of God.

We still had the knowledge that God would never give us more than we could bear.

We still had each other, our friends and our family.

We still had God's abundant mercies.

We still had the peace of God that surpasses comprehension, even in the midst of sorrows.

We still had a wonderful eternity with Him to look forward to...and so much more!

It has been seven years since Craig was diagnosed. Although we continually remember and thank the LORD for many blessings, we find that we now rarely consider the things which are gone. We have learned much from several biblical figures, including the apostle Paul, who wrote:

> *"But what things were gain to me, these I have counted loss for Christ."*
> Philippians 3:7

> *"...forgetting those things which are behind and reaching forward*
> *to those things which are ahead, I press on toward the goal..."*
> Philippians 3:13-14

Today, Craig is doing well. He is still on medication, but life is, for the most part, "normal." Craig has become an accomplished musician, both instrumentally and vocally. (Yes, I'm a mom speaking—but it's true!) He has just started his freshman year of college and plans to major in music in the area of saxophone performance. I asked him a few days ago if he had any thoughts to share for this story. He said, "No, not really. I just don't think about Crohn's much." What a testimony to God's sufficiency and grace!

God of Grace,

Help me to keep my eyes on You as I go through life.
Thank You for Your Word that gives me truths and promises by which to live.
Teach and encourage me, I pray.

PART ONE

I will abide in _____ _____ *forever .*
I will trust in the shelter of _____ _____ ."
Psalm _____ :4

"To everything there is a season,
a time for every purpose under heaven:

A time to be born,
And a time to die...

A time to weep,
And a time to laugh;

A time to mourn,
And a time to dance...

A time to gain,
And a time to lose..."

Ecclesiastes 3:1-2a, 4, 6a

*L*osses in life are inevitable. Often, they are accompanied by grief, mourning and tears.

Although depression can have many varied causes, the way we respond to the losses of life will determine (to a great extent) the degree of difficulty we have with depression.

1. Take a few moments to record some of life's "losses" that can result in feelings of depression.
Put a star by any you have personally experienced.

2. Some of the losses you recorded in Question 1 may have been:

Loss of the life of a loved one   Loss of a home or treasured possession

Loss of health   Loss of companionship / friendship / love

Loss of employment or financial security   Loss of an opportunity.

Some of life's losses are not as easily identifiable; however, they are still capable of resulting in feelings of depression. For example:

Loss of relationship / fellowship / peace with God   Loss of a personal hope or dream

Loss of personal freedom   Loss of a loved one's hope or dream

Loss of popularity or feelings of acceptance   Loss of purity / virginity

Loss of believing that life is "fair"   Loss of control

Loss of a former state of life   Loss of the feeling of being needed.

3. Loss is normal. Sorrow over loss is normal...even biblical. Neither loss nor sorrow leads directly to depression. However, *focusing* on losses *in unbiblical ways* can quickly lead to depression. Grief and sadness are part of life; but long-term, self-focused grief and sadness (in which one's focus on God dims and hope that joy will come again diminishes), are unbiblical responses to loss. These *do* cause depression.

Give some serious thought as to how you would rate your experience with depression caused by the loss of something—and then place an X in the appropriate place on one or (if applicable) both lines in the statements which follow.

a. A typical statement about depression in my life would look most like:

Although I have had   My problem with   My problem with
many losses and do have   depression due to   depression due to
times of normal grief   loss is periodic.   loss is ongoing.
and sadness, I do not
tend toward depression
related to loss.

b. When I do experience depression due to loss, it is usually:

| Mild | Problematic | Heavy | Intense | Debilitating |

4. In order to learn how to think about and deal with losses biblically, consider the following three basic categories of losses:

Those that are not or need not be permanent (even if they seem so)
Those that sometimes are and sometimes are not permanent
Those that are permanent (at least for this life)

God's Word, either by direct teaching or in principle, teaches us how to deal with each of these. The rest of today's study will focus on the first type of loss.

Losses that are not or need not be permanent

The major loss in this category is the loss of relationship, fellowship, or peace with God.

If you have ever thought that the LORD could not or would not forgive you for some sin(s), then consider the greatness of His forgiveness in the lives of Manessah (2 Chronicles 33:1-20) and Paul (1 Timothy 1:12-17.)

If you say, "Well, of course God forgave them. They weren't believers when they committed their sins," then remember David (2 Samuel 12:1-9, 13).

Finish the following statement using only one word: My relationship with the LORD at this time is...
(Possible answers would include: peaceful, estranged, variable, etc.)

5. Isaiah 44:22 is a wonderful verse written to the nation of Israel but applicable to all God's people. Israel was to turn from sinful ways and return to the LORD...and this is the call to all of God's people. Jesus Christ paid the price for your sin.

If Christ is your Savior, then when you have lost fellowship and peace with God, you need only to turn from your sin (confess and repent) and return to the LORD!

As you read Isaiah 44:22-23, answer the following questions:

a. How does God describe what He has done with the sins of His people?

b. Why were His people to return to Him? (v. 22b)

c. What is nature called on to do when the people of God return to Him? (v. 23)

d. God gives other assurances of His forgiveness in many different word pictures. In the verses below, underline the various phrases which describe how He treats the sins of His people.

*" As far as the east is from the west,
so far has He removed our transgressions from us."*

"...For You have cast all my sins behind Your back."
*[lit. the idea of the middle of the back
(between the shoulder blades)...where they cannot be seen!]*

*"Who is a God like You, pardoning iniquity...
You will cast all our sins into the depths of the sea."*

Psalm 103:12, Isaiah 38:17, Micah 7:18-19

6. Through Scripture, God's people can know that He forgives all sin and always desires our return and repentance. Look at some believers who acted upon what they knew.

   a. The book of Hosea recounts a people who have gone astray from the LORD. It also states the affliction God designs in response to their sin.

      1) Read Hosea 4:1-2. Record the sins with which the LORD charged His people.

      2) Read Hosea 5:15-6:3. Note God's reason for allowing His people to experience affliction. (5:15)

      3) How do God's people respond? Do they say, "We can't return, it's been too long," or "He'll never forgive us," or "Let's not return today...maybe later," or something else? (6:1)

      4) What is their plan of action as they return to God? (6:3a)

   b. Now consider the words of David after he committed sins including adultery, murder and deception and discovered that he was no longer in fellowship or at peace with God.

      1) Read Psalm 51 and record at least three phrases which show that David had returned to the LORD in repentance and humility.

      2) What does David pray for and expect in verses 12 and 15?

      3) What does David know about God that is the basis for his expectation of restored joy? (v. 16-17)

7. In small ways, every believer must be conscious of the daily need to return to the LORD, to confess sin as soon as it is known and to re-commit to living humbly under the loving hand of God. When we do not do this regularly and from the heart, we may begin to experience the feeling of distance from God. In these instances, we must remember that He is waiting for our return, orchestrating events to cause us to seek Him again. Any hard things that come into our lives are not because He has left us, but because He desires us to humble ourselves and submit to His sovereign care and rule.

Will you make a deeper commitment to pursue the knowledge of the LORD? If you have strayed (whether a little or a lot), will you return now?

PART TWO

I will _____ _____ Your tabernacle forever.

I will _____ _____ the _____ of Your wings."

Psalm _____ :4

*T*his part focuses on:

Losses that sometimes are and sometimes are not permanent

Of all the categories, this list is the longest and most varied. The way you handle these losses is crucial!

1. Look back at the list of losses in Part One and record at least six losses that could be, but would not necessarily be, permanent and write these below. For example: the loss of health is sometimes permanent, yet in many instances it is restored completely.

2. How does God want us to think about losses such as these? Are there any direct teachings? Are there examples given from godly people who have experienced loss? An extensive study is not possible in a short amount of time, but record your thoughts as you read the following overview passages.

   a. Use the following verses to determine some of the thoughts, actions, attitudes and emotions that would be biblical in a time of lost health.

   1) **Luke 5:31**

   2) **2 Corinthians 12:7-10** *(The exact nature of Paul's "thorn" is not stated, but the principles still apply.)*

   3) Philippians 2:25-30

   4) Hebrews 11:21-22

   b. In the loss of personal hopes, dreams, or opportunities, the following thoughts and attitudes enable a biblical response:

   1) **Philippians 3:12-14**

   2) Hebrews 11:17-19

c. In the loss of status/prestige/position, the following attitudes and understandings are essential:

   1) **Philippians 3:4-9**

   2) Philippians 3:20-4:1

d. In the loss of personal freedom, have these attitudes of Paul:

   1) **Philippians 1:12-14**

   2) **Philippians 4:11-13**

e. In the loss of a former state of life ("life as I know it"), the following examples reveal reactions that are pleasing to God. Record **what the following people lost** (or were about to lose) along with **how they responded to the change** in "life as they knew it."

   1) **Abraham**—*(If needed, see Hebrews 11:8-10)*

   2) **Noah**—*(If needed, see Genesis 8:15-20)*

   3) **Joseph**—*(If needed, see Genesis 45:4-8, 50:19)*

   4) **The Disciples**—*(If needed, see Matthew 4:18-22)*

   5) **Mary**—*(If needed, see Luke 1:30-38)*

3. The losses in your life may be because of sin on your part, or they may simply be because you live in a fallen world. Either way, have you responded to them in a biblical manner?

In every loss you experience, will you ask God to give you:

The eternal outlook of Abraham

The worshipful spirit of Noah

The trusting faith of Joseph

The willing feet of the disciples

The servant heart of Mary

The attitudes of Paul

and

The ultimate desire of the Israelites to return to the LORD and pursue the knowledge of Him?

PART THREE

_____ _____ *abide in Your tabernacle* _____ .

_____ _____ _____ *in the shelter of Your wings."*

Psalm _____ :4

The last category to consider is perhaps the hardest of all:

Losses that are permanent (at least for this world)

A special note to those who have suffered great loss:
   I know this lesson may have been hard for you—and this third part may be harder still. If you need
   to put it aside for a time, or wait and complete it with someone who is discipling you, do so.
   It is crucial that you grasp the truths ahead in order to honor God in your loss and overcome any
   depression that has put down roots; however, you may need to study these truths in small "doses."
   I have asked God to give you grace, strength, encouragement, wisdom and peace as you study.
   Will you ask Him to do the same?

Also note that although you will study the following principles in relation to losses that are permanent, they apply to every type of loss.

May the LORD bless your study.

1. God gives us many directions and encouragements for times of loss. Some are through direct teaching, and others are by the example of believers who have suffered loss. The following truths are essential to understand.

a. **God understands the depths of heartache and suffering.** Circle the words in the following verses which cause you to know this.

1) Isaiah 53:3-5

"He is despised and rejected by men, a Man of sorrows and acquainted with grief...He was despised, and we did not esteem Him. Surely He has borne our griefs and carried our sorrows; yet we esteemed Him stricken, smitten by God, and afflicted. But He was wounded for our transgressions, He was bruised for our iniquities...by His stripes we are healed."

2) John 11:32-35

"Then, when Mary came where Jesus was, and saw Him she fell down at His feet, saying to Him, 'Lord, if You had been here, my brother would not have died.' Therefore, when Jesus saw her weeping, and the Jews who came with her weeping, He groaned in the spirit and was troubled. And He said, 'Where have you laid him?' They said to Him, 'Lord, come and see.' Jesus wept."

b. **Believers will experience sorrow, but not just any kind of sorrow.** 1 Thessalonians 4:13-14 says:

"But I do not want you to be ignorant, brethren, concerning those who have fallen asleep, lest you sorrow as others who have no hope. For if we believe that Jesus died and rose again, even so God will bring with Him those who sleep in Jesus."

1) Fill in the blank: Sorrow but do so with _____.

2) King David experienced the sorrow of losing an infant son.

   a) From 2 Samuel 12:16-23, would you say he sorrowed with or without hope?
   Record his actions and words to explain your answer.

   b) *(Optional)* The death of a child is one of the hardest losses to suffer. A letter by Samuel Rutherford, a Scottish Puritan pastor, has brought great encouragement to my heart. It is in Appendix D, should you wish to read it.

c. **Even when a loss is due to personal sin, God delights to show lovingkindness.** (Jeremiah 9:24) One way He does this is to abundantly restore favor. (Hosea 6:1-3) Believers will suffer consequences for sin—even permanent consequences—however, they stand forgiven, and God will work to bring them to repentance and restoration of His favor. God did this with David in 2 Samuel 12.

Although David's child died as a consequence of his sin, David did not remain under God's hard discipline forever. Though God does not always demonstrate His forgiveness, lovingkindness and restored favor in this way, how did He show it to a repentant David in 2 Samuel 12:24-25?

d. **You will never suffer alone.** Isaiah 63:7-9a says:

"I will mention the lovingkindness of the LORD...For He said, 'Surely they are My people...'
So He became their Savior. In all their affliction He was afflicted..."

1) Underline the words in this passage that tell you that the LORD always suffers with His people.

2) Circle the word "all." Why is it significant? What does it tell you?

e. **The losses of this life are under the control of a sovereign God.** As you have studied already, nothing can or will thwart the plans that God has for His people and eternity.

1) In Jeremiah 29:11 God speaks to the people of Israel and says:

"'For I know the plans I have for you,' declares the LORD,
'plans to prosper you and not to harm you,
plans to give you hope and a future.'"

Draw a box around the things His plans will do.

2) God has plans for all His people. (Psalm 33:11) If, in a time of loss and sorrow, you do not see how God's plans could possibly prosper you, what should you do? *(Review the introduction to Lesson Five, Part Two, if needed.)*

f. **It is essential to come to the place where you can give thanks to God** for Who He is and what He has accomplished in your life through life's struggles and sorrows.

"...in everything give thanks;
for this is the will of God in Christ Jesus for you."
1 Thessalonians 5:18

1) Circle the phrase in the verse above that tells why we must give thanks in *everything*.

2) Why would giving thanks in everything (including every loss) be so essential that God would specifically state it to be His will for you? [Give some thought to this. The following verses may offer additional insight: Romans 1:21 and 2 Timothy 3:1-5 (especially the last part of verse 2)]

3) How does someone give thanks "in" a loss?

4) What are some things that might keep someone from giving thanks in a loss?

g. **God understands how difficult it can be to give thanks.** As you read Hebrews 13:15, underline the word "sacrifice."

> *"Therefore by Him let us continually offer the sacrifice of praise to God,*
> *that is, the fruit of our lips, giving thanks to His name."*

1) Read Hebrews 13:15 again. Did you notice the "that is" that connects the sacrifice of praise and the giving thanks? Underline the phrase about giving thanks.

2) Are there circumstances of your life for which you have yet to give thanks? Yes_____ No_____

    a) If there are any circumstances in which you have not been willing to give thanks, will you, with the strength only God can give, pray the words of the LORD's people and return to Your LORD this day?

> *"Come and let us return to the LORD;*
> *For He has torn, but He will heal us;*
> *He has stricken, but He will bind us up...Let us know,*
> *Let us pursue the knowledge of the LORD."*
>
> Isaiah 6:1-3

    Will you trust Him with your life? Yes_____ No_____

    b) Again, it is not easy to give thanks to God in our losses. But if we choose not to humbly offer the sacrifice of thanksgiving to our sovereign, loving, holy, merciful, gracious, faithful, caring LORD, then we are placing our feelings above the commandments of the LORD and are, in effect, saying "You are wrong. This will not prosper me. This will not work for my good. You should not have allowed it. I know better than You."

    Is that your intent? May it never be so!

h. **It is important not to let your losses "run amok,"** consuming your thoughts, increasing your worries and playing havoc with your emotions. God gives grace to persevere for the present day. His grace is always sufficient. Since you do not know what the future will bring, don't try to imagine how you will ever be able to live without that which you have lost. God will take care of giving you the needed grace for each day as it comes.

Fill in the blanks below.

1) *"Give us _____ _____ our daily bread."* Matthew 6:11

2) *"...choose yourselves _____ _____ whom you will serve."* Joshua 24:15

3) *"_____ is the _____ the LORD has made..."* Psalm 118:24

"Do not worry about tomorrow, for tomorrow will worry about its own things." (Matthew 6:34)
Live this day. Serve this day. Offer yourself this day to the LORD's service. Grace abounds for you this day. Tomorrow, when it comes, will be "this day," and all God's promises and provisions will be there for you!

Thought for meditation:

What do you do when you have responded biblically to a loss, and to the best of your ability you are:

> holding to an eternal perspective
>
> offering worship from the heart, including the sacrifices of praise and thanksgiving
>
> humbly submitting to God's plans for your life
>
> continually seeking to live a life that will bring honor and glory to God...

yet the loss keeps coming to mind and bringing fresh tears and heartache. What do you do? Think on this for a moment before you look below for my thoughts.

1. I believe that God would tell you to go ahead and cry. He designed tears for a purpose, and as a grieving father put it:

> "The old tears were wept again, but through them God made the rainbow to shine."[1]

And do not feel that you ever cry alone: God knows and cares about every tear. (Psalm 56:8)

2. Grieve, but be sure you do not grieve as the world does. Grieve with hope. In your grief, by word and deed, give evidence of your faith and hope. In other words, acknowledge God (His character and His ways) and show your hope by going on with life. If God kept you on this earth, He has more for you to do than grieve all the way to your death! Many of God's commands remind us to "press on" and "focus on the things above," etc. Remember, it does not dishonor a loved one who is gone when you put aside grief to honor and obey the LORD by living life fully and obediently.

3. When fresh grief comes, remind yourself of the truths and promises of God (over and over, if necessary). Turn your eyes from your loss and grief to God. Concentrate on Him. Recall His names, His promises, His works and the bright eternity where He will wipe away every tear and there will be no more sorrow or crying. Return from a focus on your loss to your LORD! (Revelation 21:4)

The day of complete peace and joy will come! This day, serve Him!

Thoughts, Meditations and Prayers

Jehovah-Shalom The LORD is Peace

*T*he first mention of Jehovah-Shalom, the LORD is Peace, is found in the book of Judges in the narrative about Gideon. Why did Gideon need to know that the LORD was his peace? What can we learn from his circumstance?

1. Gideon and the people of the LORD had been in the hand of the Midianites for several years. Read about this in Judges 6:1-6.

   a. Record the conditions God's people were facing.

   b. Record the length of time these conditions had been affecting the people of the LORD. (6:1)

2. The people had lost a right relationship with God (6:1). They had also lost their security, prosperity and freedom. If you read on in Judges 6, you will find that the LORD instructs a hesitant and reluctant Gideon to go up against the Midianites to defeat them.

   a. What are the instructions and promises God gave to Gideon in verses 14-16?

   b. Why did Gideon not feel capable of doing what the LORD instructed? (6:15)

   c. As God increased Gideon's faith, Gideon built an altar to the LORD. Read verses 22-24 and record the name of the altar.

   d. Given Gideon's circumstances and God's commission and promises, why might Gideon have called the altar "The LORD Is Peace"?

3. There are two main ways Scripture describes the peace that comes from God. Read the two passages below and fill in the blanks.

Peace _____ God

Romans 5:1

How we get this peace:

1) _____

2) _____

Regarding peace **with** God, Pastor John MacArthur says, "Not a subjective, internal sense of calm and serenity, but an external, objective reality. God has declared Himself to be at war with every human being because of man's sinful rebellion against Him and His laws... But the first great result of justification is that the sinner's war with God is ended forever (Col. 1:21-22). Scripture refers to the end of this conflict as a person's being reconciled to God."[10]

Peace _____ God

Philippians 4:6-9

How we get this peace (4:6b, 8-9):

_____

_____

How it is described:

_____

What it does:

_____

MacArthur says the following about the peace **of** God: "Inner calm or tranquility is promised to the believer who has a thankful attitude based on unwavering confidence that God is able and willing to do what is best for His children."[11]

Has God granted each of these kinds of peace in your own life? Explain fully...and if you have never experienced peace *with* God (salvation), now is the time!

4. On the following pages you will find several verses on peace written down the left hand column of each page. Read the verses, marking a capital *P* over the word peace each time you see it. Then, record what you learn about true peace in the space provided *(four are completed for you)*.

Scriptures

a. *"Great peace have those who love Your law, and nothing causes them to stumble."*
Psalm 119:165

b. *"You will keep him in perfect peace, whose mind is stayed on You, because he trusts in You."*
Isaiah 26:3

c. *"For to be carnally minded is death, but to be spiritually minded is life and peace."*
Romans 8:6

Peace is the result of being spiritually minded

d. *"...Be of good comfort, be of one mind, live in peace; and the God of love and peace will be with you."* 2 Corinthians 13:11

e. *"But now in Christ Jesus you who once were far off have been brought near by the blood of Christ. For He Himself is our peace, who has made both one, and has broken down the middle wall of separation, having abolished in His flesh the enmity...so as to create in Himself one new man from the two, thus making peace, and that He might reconcile them both to God in one body through the cross, thereby putting to death the enmity."* Ephesians 2:13-16

f. *"For the mountains shall depart and the hills be removed, but my kindness shall not depart from you, nor shall My covenant of peace be removed."* Isaiah 54:10

g. *"The LORD will give strength to His people; the LORD will bless His people with peace."*
Psalm 29:11

Peace is a blessing from the LORD
It is for His people

h. *"Depart from evil and do good; Seek peace and pursue it."* Psalm 34:14

i. "*And you, who once were alienated and enemies in your mind by wicked works, yet now He has reconciled [made peace] in the body of His flesh through death, to present you holy, and blameless, and above reproach in His sight.*" Colossians 1:21-22

j. "*...let the peace of God rule in your hearts, to which also you were called in one body; and be thankful.*" Colossians 3:15

k. [Jesus speaking] "*Peace I leave with you, My peace I give to you; not as the world gives do I give to you. Let not your heart be troubled, neither let it be afraid. You have heard Me say to you, 'I am going away and coming back to you'...*" John 14:27-28

There is a peace that the world gives—it is not the kind of peace Christ gives

Christ's peace is for His followers (those for whom He is coming back)

Christ left peace with us

l. [Jesus speaking] "*These things I have spoken to you, that in Me you may have peace. In the world you will have tribulation; but be of good cheer, I have overcome the world.*" John 16:33

m. "*...so it may not happen, when he hears the words of this curse, that he blesses himself in his heart, saying, 'I shall have peace, even though I follow the dictates of my heart'—as though the drunkard could be included with the sober.*" Deuteronomy 29:19

Peace is not the result of going your own way ("following your heart.")

n. "*Now may the God of hope fill you with all joy and peace in believing, that you may abound in hope by the power of the Holy Spirit.*" Romans 15:13

o. "*But the fruit of the Spirit is love, joy, peace...*" Galatians 5:22

5. From what you have studied, does God simply grant peace or does man have a responsibility to pursue it?

    a. If man has a responsibility, what does it include?

    b. Can man have peace without God graciously granting it to him? Explain.

6. What truths do you think are most essential to pass on to the next generation about peace with God and the peace of God?

7. An old hymn connects the peace man so desires with the presence and heart of God. Read the words out loud. (Of course, sing if you know the tune!)

> **There is a place of quiet rest, Near to the heart of God,**
> **A place where sin cannot molest, Near to the heart of God.**
>
> O Jesus, blest Redeemer, Sent from the heart of God,
> Hold us who wait before Thee, Near to the heart of God.
>
> **There is a place of comfort sweet, Near to the heart of God.**
> **A place where we our Savior meet, Near to the heart of God.**
>
> O Jesus, blest Redeemer, Sent from the heart of God,
> Hold us who wait before Thee, Near to the heart of God.
>
> **There is a place of full release, Near to the heart of God.**
> **A place where all is joy and peace, Near to the heart of God.**
>
> O Jesus, blest Redeemer, Sent from the heart of God,
> Hold us who wait before Thee, Near to the heart of God.[12]

Would you make the chorus of this hymn your prayer today as you tell God that you know that only in Him can you find true and lasting peace?

147

Thoughts, Meditations and Prayers

Getting the Picture

"I have set the LORD always before me;
Because He is at my right hand I shall not be moved.
Therefore my heart is glad, and my glory rejoices;
My flesh also will rest in hope."
Psalm 16:8-9

*G*od gives us many pictures throughout Scripture that help us "see" Him and His provision for us. Studying the passages that picture the provision of the LORD is a blessing that increases hope! Enjoy!

1. Below are some of the wonderful word pictures found in Scripture.

Look up the initial verse, recording the appropriate word in each blank.
Write out one phrase or portion of the verse that contains the word picture.
Complete the assignments which follow.

a. **1 John 1:5**   God is _____.
Portion of the verse containing the word picture:

Read the following verses that refer to God as light. Underline phrases or truths to remember.

1)   *"...The LORD my God will enlighten my darkness."* Psalm 18:28b

2)   *"Your word is a lamp to my feet and a light to my path."* Psalm 119:105

3)   *"Then Jesus spoke...saying, 'I am the light of the world. He who follows Me shall not walk in darkness, but have the light of life.'"* John 8:12

Light is essential for life. What specific things is it essential for...and how does the truth that God is light give you insight into His provision for you?

b. **Jeremiah 2:13**   God is the _____ of living _____

Portion of the verse containing the word picture:

In the following verses, underline phrases that refer to God as a fountain.

1) *"They are abundantly satisfied with the fullness of Your house,*
   And You give them drink from the river of Your pleasures.
   For with You is the fountain of life; in Your light we see light." Psalm 36:8-9

2) *"The LORD will guide you continually, and satisfy your soul in drought...*
   you shall be like a watered garden, and like a spring of water, whose waters do not fail."

   Isaiah 58:11

3) *"[Jesus answered] but whoever drinks of the water that I shall give him will never thirst.*
   But the water that I shall give him will become in him a fountain of water springing up
   into everlasting life." John 4:14

> What insights are there in having a LORD who is a fountain of water? Consider all you know about fountains and water as you answer.

c. **Genesis 15:1**   God describes Himself as a _____, Abraham's exceedingly great reward.

Portion of the verse containing the word picture:

As you read the following verses, mark words that refer to God as a shield.

1) *"For You...will bless the righteous; with favor You will surround him as with a shield."*

   Psalm 5:12 (cross-reference with Job 1:9-10)

2) *"His truth shall be your shield and buckler."* Psalm 91:4b (cross-reference with Proverbs 30:5)

3) *"You have also given me the shield of Your salvation..."* 2 Samuel 22:36a (see also Psalm 18:35)

4) *"...taking the shield of faith with which you will be able to quench all the fiery darts of the*
   wicked one." Ephesians 6:16

Record the purpose(s) of a shield.

According to the Scriptures, in addition to God Himself, what are some of God's provisions that serve or act as a shield for believers?

d. **Psalm 3:3**   God is described as the one who _____ the head

Portion of the verse containing the word picture:

When God lifts our heads, what might He want us to see? Underline the answers you find.

1) *"I will lift up my eyes to the hills—from whence comes my help? My help comes from the LORD who made heaven and earth."* Psalm 121:1-2

2) *"Unto You I lift up my eyes, O You who dwell in the heavens. Behold, as the eyes of servants look to the hand of their masters...so our eyes look to the LORD our God..."* Psalm 123:1-2

3) *"The LORD upholds all who fall, and raises up all who are bowed down. The eyes of all look expectantly to You...You open Your hand and satisfy the desire of every living thing."*
Psalm 145:14-16

4) *"In that day a man will look to his Maker, and his eyes will have respect for the Holy One of Israel..."* Isaiah 17:7

5) *"Lift up your eyes on high, and see who has created these things, who brings out their host by number"* Isaiah 40:26

6) *"Therefore we do not lose heart...while we do not look at the things which are seen, but at the things which are not seen. For the things which are seen are temporary, but the things which are not seen are eternal."* 2 Corinthians 4:16-18 (see also Colossians 3:1-4)

When you feel bowed down and low, what help or insight does the picture of God as the lifter of your head give you?

2.   Of the word pictures you have studied, which has meant the most to you or given you the most encouragement for your life today? Why?

3.   Which picture could you best use to encourage a family member, friend or one you disciple? What would you say?

4.   End your study time in conversation with the LORD. If you would like, you may begin praying by using a portion of the verses you began with:

"I have set the LORD always before me;
Because He is at my right hand I shall not be moved.
Therefore my heart is glad, and my glory rejoices;
My flesh also will rest in hope."

Psalm 16:8-9

Father, today I have set You before me as I have studied some of the word pictures You have provided. The picture of You as _____ has made my heart glad, caused me to rejoice and increased my hope in You. Help me to always keep this picture in mind, especially in times of...

Thoughts, Meditations and Prayers

Hear my cry, O God;
Attend to my prayer.

From the end of the earth I will cry to You,
When my heart is overwhelmed;
Lead me to the rock that is higher than I.

For You have been a shelter for me,
A strong tower from the enemy.

I will abide in Your tabernacle forever;
I will trust in the shelter of Your wings.

Psalm 61:1-4

Lesson Seven

From Here To Eternity

*"Let us therefore come boldly to the throne of grace,
that we may obtain mercy and find grace to help in time of need."*

Hebrews 4:16

During my early teenage years, my mom and dad bought a loveseat to put in their bedroom. We sat on this small sofa to read, watch television, talk, cry (and they would put their arms around me), make plans, get help with homework and just enjoy being together.

I was always welcome in their room. When I was there, I felt secure and loved.

I grew up and left home; but every time I return for a visit, it's still my favorite place to go.

Over the years, many people have been invited to my parents' home...but they were not invited into their bedroom. Only members of our family are comfortable there. When I got married, my husband also came to love visiting with the family in my parents' room. The small sofa is now one of his favorite places, too.

Perhaps you have such a place in the home you grew up in. If not, perhaps you wish you did.

You do have such a place in Heaven. Every Christian has a heavenly Father who has such a room—a throne room—and everyone in His family is welcome there. If you are His child, He bids you to come to Him: He calls you to come boldly before the throne of grace. He asks you to stay, to talk with Him, to tell Him your hurts and your joys. He understands what it is to suffer, and He asks you to cast all your cares upon Him. He cares for you.

Your Father's arms are open wide to comfort you, to uphold you, to encourage you, to rejoice with you.

Unlike earthly parents, He is sufficient for every problem.

Unlike earthly parents, He is perfect—in His ways and in His love.

The doors to His throne room are open to all His children. They are always open. Because the One on the throne is your Father, you are always welcome in His presence.

Father,

You have opened the way to the throne of Heaven
and bid me to come.
This shows me the love You have for me.
Help me show my love for You as I respond rightly to Your Word.

PART ONE

Hear my _____, O God; Attend to my _____.

From the end of the _____ I will cry to You,

When _____ heart is overwhelmed;

Lead me to the _____ that is _____ than I.

For _____ have been a shelter for me,

A strong tower from the _____.

I will _____ in _____ tabernacle _____;

I will _____ in the shelter of Your wings.

Psalm 61:1-4

As we live in the "here and now" of this world, one of the thoughts we must keep firmly rooted in our minds is that our:

"...faith and hope are in God."

1 Peter 1:21

Hope is for the here and now; it sees us through to the time when we will meet our Lord face to face. Since our hope lies in God alone, we must go to Him in dependence, faith and expectation. We must go to Him for help, understanding, encouragement, direction, strength, and protection. And we must go, not once, but continuously.

One of the most gracious and comforting verses in all of Scripture is Hebrews 4:16. It says:

"Let us therefore come boldly to the throne of grace,
that we may obtain mercy and find grace to help in time of need."

1. Since God is our hope and we are bid to come "boldly" (with freedom, confidence...without fear or hesitation) to God's throne, perhaps some inquiries about God's throne would be helpful (and exciting!). For example:

"What is God's throne like?" "How is it described?" "Where is it?" "Who can come to His throne?"

"How often can I come to His throne?" "What can I expect?" "How do I approach the throne?"

If you can think of more questions, write them below.

2. Complete the chart below by making brief notes on the following passages:

Psalm 89:14   **Daniel 7:9-10**   **Hebrews** 1:8, **4:16**

Isaiah 6:1-7   Matthew 19:27-30, 25:31-32   **Revelation 3:21, 4:1-3, 5:11-14**

(Be sure to indicate the verse from which you get each of your entries.)

The Throne of God

How it is Described   *What Takes Place There*

3. What is your reaction to God's invitation to "come boldly" to His throne?

PART TWO

> Hear my cry, _____ _____; _____ to my prayer.
>
> From the end of the earth I will _____ _____ _____ ,
>
> When my heart is overwhelmed;
>
> _____ me to the rock that is _____ _____ ____.
>
> For You have been a shelter for me,
>
> A _____ _____ from the enemy.
>
> I will abide in Your tabernacle forever;
>
> I will trust in the _____ of Your _____.
>
> Psalm ____:1-4

God's throne is a throne of power, might, righteousness, justice and holiness. Thankfully, it is also a throne of grace and mercy; if it were not, man would have no grounds for hope and no admittance to the throne.

1. How can an eternal, holy, all-powerful, transcendent God who created all things and sits on His throne in the heavens possibly help, understand, and sympathize with our frailties, sufferings and weaknesses? Read Hebrews 4:14-16 and answer the questions that follow.

   a. Who is man's great High Priest? (v. 14)

   b. It is significant that two titles (or names) are used in this passage when referring to our High Priest: one emphasizes His humanity, the other, His deity. Which is which?

      "Jesus" emphasizes His _____.

      "Son of God" emphasizes His _____.

   c. What is Jesus the Son of God able to do? (v. 15)

      1) Why is He able to sympathize with the weaknesses of man? (v. 15)

      2) In how many ways is man tempted that Christ was not tempted? (v. 15b)

Record at least four things about Jesus as our High Priest from Hebrews 2:17-18.

a. What are some of the things God experienced in the person of Jesus Christ that helps Him sympathize with us now?

1) Mark 14:32-36 is the account of Christ in Gethsemane. Circle the words in verses 33 and 34 that describe the emotions Jesus experienced.

> *33 "And He took Peter, James, and John with Him,*
> *and He began to be troubled and deeply distressed.*
> *34 Then He said to them, 'My soul is exceedingly sorrowful, even to death...'"*

2) You looked at Isaiah 53:3-4 in the last lesson. As you read it again, circle each occurrence of the words "we" and "our."

> *"He is despised and rejected by men,*
> *A Man of sorrows and acquainted with grief.*
> *And we hid, as it were, our faces from Him;*
> *He was despised, and we did not esteem Him.*
> *Surely He has borne our griefs and carried our sorrows;*
> *Yet we esteemed Him stricken, smitten by God, and afflicted."*

b. What makes Jesus the Son of God different from other high priests who had acted as mediators between God and man? These are hope-giving truths—take time to savor them!

1) Hebrews 7:23-25

2) Hebrews 7:26-27

3) Hebrews 10:11-14 *[The fact that He is seated makes Him different, but the place that He is seated is awesome! Be sure to note the location! (verse 12, along with Hebrews 8:1 and 12:2)]*

160

3.   What truth stands out most in your mind about Jesus Christ as High Priest?

4.   *(Apply what you have learned to at least two of the following categories.)* What difference should the truths you have just studied make:

   In your hope?

   In your prayers?

   In your ability to persevere in hard times?

   In discipling or encouraging others?

5.   Go now to the throne of grace and thank God for the access He has provided through your great High Priest, Jesus the Son of God. Thank Him for the help He has provided. Thank Him for becoming man and coming to earth so that He can sympathize with you.

PART THREE

_____ my cry, O God; Attend to _____ _____.

From _____ _____ of the _____ I will cry to You,

When my _____ is _____;

_____ me to the _____ that is _____ than ____.

For _____ have been a _____ for _____,

A strong _____ _____ the _____.

I _____ _____ in Your _____ forever;

I _____ _____ in the shelter of _____ _____.

Psalm _____ : ____ - ____

*G*od bids us to come boldly to His throne of grace to find help in times of need. Yet, too often, we do not go to Him. We may neglect or avoid prayer for days, weeks or even months.

Knowing what God has done to open the way into His presence, and knowing what He says about Himself and His throne, this seems incomprehensible: why would God's child *not* run to His throne room? Why would God's child *not* go to the Father?

This last section of study takes a brief look at three things that may keep God's children from coming in prayer to their Father's throne. These are crucial to identify, for if they keep us from going to the God of all hope, then we will begin to despair.

Three things that may keep a believer away from God's throne are:

Guilt

Bitterness

Unbalanced affections

Before you take a closer look at these three, can you think of other things that might keep a believer from coming to God's throne in prayer?

Has *Guilt* **Kept You From the Throne?**

1. There are many things that can cause both believers and non-believers to have ongoing feelings of guilt; three prominent ones are premarital sex, divorce and abortion. Can you think of others?

2. It is VITAL to understand God's purpose and cure for a guilty conscience. God puts a conscience within every man. This is an instinctive sense of right and wrong that warns the soul that it is about to, or that it already has, transgressed God's laws. It becomes active when thoughts of sinful activity enter the mind. If it is not desensitized (1 Timothy 4:2) or misinformed, it will remain active until it accomplishes its purpose of bringing a person to the point of repentance and restoration of a right relationship with God and others.

   a. What kind of a conscience does God desire for us to have as Christians? (If needed, see 1 Timothy 1:5, 2 Timothy 1:3 and Acts 24:16 for your answer.)

   b. What remedy has God provided for a guilty conscience? (Use 1 John 1:8-10 and Psalm 32:5-6a in your answer.)

   c. How long do you think God desires (and designed) man to live with a guilty conscience? Why?

3. In many passages, God promises total and complete forgiveness to those who come to Him in repentance. If, as a believer, your conscience continues to accuse you even *after* you turn from your sin in confession and repentance, then what must you do?

   a. Ensure that your repentance is genuine and from the heart. Examine your motives, your confession, and the completeness of your commitment to leave that sin behind.

   b. THIS IS CRUCIAL: If you find your repentance to be genuine, but you still have feelings of guilt, then you must remind yourself again and again of God's promises to believers regarding sin. It is NOT a matter of "forgiving yourself," but of "living by what you know, not by what you feel." As you remind yourself of the truth (over and over and over again) your emotions will eventually follow! What truth? Record what you learn from the following verses.

     1) Psalm 103:12 (see also Psalm 32:1-2)

     2) Isaiah 43:25 and 44:22

     3) Hebrews 10:17 (If God doesn't, then why would we?)

   c. Remember the words of Jesus to the woman caught in adultery. He said, "Neither do I condemn you; go and sin no more." Where there is no condemnation from God (Romans 8:1), do not allow a misguided conscience to accuse you and keep you away from His throne of power and grace!

1. Hebrews 12:14-15 says:

> *"Pursue peace with all people, and holiness, without which no one will see the Lord:*
> *looking carefully lest anyone fall short of the grace of God;*
> *lest any **root of bitterness** springing up cause trouble, and by this many become defiled."*

   a. According to this passage, what are the consequences of allowing bitterness a place in your heart?

   b. Why might bitterness be described as a "root"?

   c. What things are you responsible to pursue? (Write them out just as the passage says it!)

2. When you have been wronged (or feel you have been wronged), what can you know that will help you pursue peace and avoid or let go of the sin of bitterness?

   a. Record what you learn from Romans 12:14-21.

   b. In these verses, does God promise to repay the wrongs done to you in a way you can see—or even in your lifetime? If not, what does He promise?

3. Galatians 5:16-17 lists two ways to go through life.

   a. What are they?

   b. A more detailed explanation of each way is in verses 19-23. Although the word "bitterness" is not directly mentioned, to which list would bitterness belong, and why?

4. Sometimes bitterness *toward God* keeps people from the throne. Why would such emotion need to be confessed as sin? *(In your answer, consider Deuteronomy 32:4, Job 1:22 and 2:10.)*

5. When you have been wronged by others, know that the One on the throne is completely just and injustice is *His* to repay. If you have let bitterness, irritation or resentment keep you from God's throne, will you go to the throne now—giving God any bitterness you carry and humbly asking Him for the peace which only He can give? If not, why not?

Have *Unbalanced Affections* **Kept You From the Throne?**

1. Many New Testament letters were written to perfect the thoughts, beliefs and actions of believers. One of the reasons James wrote his letter was because believers were becoming unbalanced in their view of the things of this world. They were valuing them in an unbiblical way.

    a. Read James 4:1-6 and record the wrong values held by the recipients of this letter.

    b. When you value (love) someone or something more than God would have you value it, what is it called?
        (If needed, see Ezekiel 14:3a)

    c. What are some biblical attitudes to have toward the things and ideas of this world?

       1) 1 John 2:15-17

       2) 1 Timothy 6:17-19

       3) Colossians 2:8

    d. How could an unbalanced and unbiblical love of worldly things keep you from coming to the throne of God in prayer? Give at least two specific examples.

    e. What is one way worldly philosophies or the traditions of men could keep you from the throne?

    f. Think carefully. Has anything/anyone in this world (including yourself) consumed your love, time, pursuit or attention and kept you from the Father's throne?

Have You Been Too Long From the Throne of God?

God issues your standing invitation to His throne in Hebrews 10:19-22.

*"Therefore, brethren, having boldness to enter the Holiest by the blood of Jesus,
by a new and living way which He consecrated for us, through the veil, that is, His flesh,
and having a High Priest over the house of God,
let us draw near with a true heart in full assurance of faith..."*

When Approaching the Throne, we Should Come...

(Underline thoughts which stand out to you as you read the following words from C. H. Spurgeon.)

"'The throne of grace.' That God is to be viewed in prayer as our Father is the aspect that is dearest to us. But we still are not to regard Him as though He were such as we are, for our Savior has qualified Our Father with the words 'which art in heaven.'

Reverently

"If in prayer we come to a throne, it is clear that our spirit should, in the first place, be one of *lowly reverence*...Familiarity there may be, but let it not be unhallowed. Boldness there should be, but let it not be impertinent...

Joyfully

"We come to a throne to be approached with *devout joyfulness*. If I find myself favored by divine grace to stand among those favored ones who frequent His courts, shall I not feel glad?...

Submissively

"Whenever this throne is approached, it should be with *complete submission*...No loyal child of God will for a moment imagine that he is to occupy the place of the King, but he bows before Him who has a right to be Lord of all. And though he utters his desire earnestly, passionately, importunately, and he pleads and pleads again, yet it is evermore with this needful reservation: 'Your will be done, my Lord; and, if I ask anything that is not in accordance with You, my inmost will is that You would be kind enough to deny me'...

Expectantly

"If it is a throne, it should be approached with *enlarged expectations*. We do not come, as it were, in prayer only to where God dispenses His favors to the poor or to the back door of the house of mercy to receive the scraps, though that were more than we deserve...Ask, therefore, after a Godlike fashion, for great things, for you are before a great throne...

Confidently

"The right spirit in which to approach the throne of grace is that of *unstaggering confidence*. Who shall doubt the King?...With God before us in all His glory, sitting on the throne of grace, will our hearts dare to say we mistrust Him?...

Sincerely

"If prayer is a coming before the throne of God, it should always be conducted with the *deepest sincerity*...when we venture into His presence, let us have a purpose there. Let us beware of playing at praying..."[1]

166

Your invitation to the throne in Hebrews 10:19-22 does not end with verse 22. Write out Hebrews 10:23 below then read the last phrase out loud.

More from Spurgeon:

"...on the throne of grace, God is again bound to us by His promises. The covenant contains in it many gracious promises, exceeding great and precious. 'Ask, and it shall be given you; seek, and ye shall find; knock, and it shall be opened unto you' (Matt. 7:7). Until God said that word or a word to that effect, it was at His own option to hear prayer or not, but it is not so now. If true prayer is offered through Jesus Christ, His truth binds Him to hear it. A man may be perfectly free, but the moment he makes a promise, he is not free to break it; and the everlasting God will not break His promise. He delights to fulfill it...

"Let us come boldly, for we bear the promise in our hearts."[2]

In Lesson One, the author of Psalm 42 asked himself why his soul was so downcast and disturbed within him. He then answered himself by way of instruction: "Hope in God." The psalmist knew where his hope was to be found and what action he must take.

So do you!

Difficult times will come, but God is faithful to His promise for strength.

Sorrowful times will come, but God is faithful to His promise for joy.

Times of failure and sin will come, but God is faithful to His promise of forgiveness.

Times of mourning will come, but God is faithful to His promise to be our portion.

Times of uncertainty will come, but God is faithful to His promise to be our good Shepherd.

Times of need will come, but God is on His throne, faithful to His promise of help.

So fall on your knees and come to the throne!

Eternal God and Gracious Father,

That you have opened access to Your throne and bid me come overwhelms my soul. What a privilege to approach You as your child. Forgive my times of neglect, doubt and self-focus. Thank You now for drawing me to You and giving me the desire for Your throne. May it ever be my delight, and may I live my life in praise of You— You are my hope!

Thoughts, Meditations and Prayers

The Lord God Omnipotent

*"And I heard, as it were, the voice of a great multitude,
as the sound of many waters and as the sound of mighty thunderings, saying,
'Alleluia!* **For the Lord God Omnipotent reigns!**
Let us be glad and rejoice and give Him glory...'"

Revelation 19:6-7a

At the same time that it is almost incomprehensible, the omnipotence of God is one of a Christian's greatest sources of hope.

In the original language, the word "omnipotent" comes from a word meaning "all" or "every," and another word meaning "power," "strength" or "dominion." Putting them together, we have the meaning of omnipotent: all-powerful, all-mighty.

1. As you read the following verses, underline or circle all you learn about the power of God.

The Power of God...

a. **1 Chronicles 29:12-13**

*"Both riches and honor come from You, and You reign over all. In Your hand is power and might;
In Your hand it is to make great and to give strength to all.
Now therefore, our God, we thank You and praise Your glorious name."*

b. Jeremiah 32:17

*"Ah, Lord GOD! Behold, You have made the heavens and the earth by Your great power
and outstretched arm. There is nothing too hard for You."*

c. **Romans 1:20**

*"For since the creation of the world His invisible attributes are clearly seen, being understood by
the things that are made, even His eternal power and Godhead..."*

d. **Ephesians 1:18-19**

*"...that you may know what is the hope of His calling...and what is the exceeding greatness
of His power toward us who believe, according to the working of His mighty power"*

e. Ephesians 3:20-21

*"Now to Him who is able to do exceedingly abundantly above all that we ask or think,
according to the power that works in us, to Him be glory..."*

2. God is omnipotent, having control over such things as the devil, disease, death, nature (including weather), the hearts of men, the leadership and continuance of nations and wealth. Of these things, which do you think man most tries to control, or wishes he could control?

    1) Why do you think man wants to control some of the things over which God alone has absolute power?

    2) Have you seen this tendency in yourself? If so, how?

3. Look briefly now at four of the things over which God alone has absolute power.

    a. **God has power over the devil:** list the words that indicate God's power over Satan and his followers.

The Devil Is...

    1) **Hebrews 2:14 and Colossians 2:15**

       "...that through death He [Christ] might destroy him who had the power of death, that is, the devil,"

       "Having disarmed principalities and powers, He made a public spectacle of them, triumphing over them in it."

    2) Can you think of some instances where God's power over the devil is displayed in Scripture?

    b. **God has power over disease and death:** what phrases tell of God's power over these things?

Regarding Life and Health, God...

    1) **Job 12:9-10 and Exodus 15:26b**
       (see also Psalm 139:16 and John 10:17-18)

       "Who among all these does not know that the hand of the LORD has done this, in whose hand is the life of every living thing, and the breath of all mankind."

       "...For I am the LORD who heals you."

    2) How is this power displayed in Mark 1:29-34, Matthew 28:5-7 and John 11:1-44?

c. **God has power over nature:** what phrases describe the extent of God's power over all of creation?

In the Realm of Nature, God...

   1) **Psalm 65**

     (If you have time, read the whole psalm, but
     only record a few phrases from verses 6-10)

   2) Can you think of some instances where Scripture tells of God's power over nature?

d. **God has power over the hearts of men** (mind, thoughts, and will): list the words that tell what abilities He has.

God Has Power
Over the Heart to...

   1) **1 Chronicles 28:9 and 29:18-19**

     "As for you, my son Solomon, know the God of your
     father, and serve Him with a loyal heart and with a
     willing mind; for the LORD searches all hearts and
     understands all the intent of the thoughts."

     "O LORD God...keep this forever in the intent
     of the thoughts of the heart of Your people,
     and fix their heart toward You.
     And give my son Solomon a loyal heart to
     keep Your commandments..."

   2) Psalm 51:10, 86:11 and 119:36

     "Create in me a clean heart, O God..."
     "...Unite my heart to fear Your name."
     "Incline my heart to Your testimonies..."

   3) **Proverbs 21:1** (see also Ezra 6:22 and 7:27)

     "The king's heart is in the hand of the LORD,
     like the rivers of water;
     He turns it wherever He wishes."

   4) **Acts 16:14**

     "Now a certain woman named Lydia heard us...
     The Lord opened her heart to heed the
     things spoken by Paul."

   5) How is God's power over the heart displayed in Ezra 1:1 and Galatians 1:13-15?

171

4. An incorrect understanding of the power of God can lead to erroneous thinking, mistaken conclusions, wrong beliefs, uncontrolled emotions and sinful actions. A correct understanding of the power of God leads to faith, trust, obedience and hope. Many Christians sing of God's power and say they know He is powerful; however, they do not always live as if He is in control. In doing so, they can ultimately become fearful, depressed, and drained by trying to control things over which they really have no control.

How would a full understanding of God's power help you respond biblically to the following? Record at least one truth about God's power relevant to each situation and then add a situation of your own.

a. a rebellious child whose heart is hardened to the LORD

b. a tornado, hurricane, flood or fire that destroys your house

c. the evil that is in the world today

d. unexpected and/or serious illness

e. a spouse that will not allow you to pursue spiritual things and service as you desire
(After you answer, see Appendix E for a letter I wrote to a young wife who faced this situation.)

f. _____

5. In order to keep a strong hope, we must consistently remember that the Lord God Omnipotent reigns!

We have hope because God limits Satan's activities now and will totally remove him in the future.
We have hope because God will heal all of His children (whether in this world or in the next, it is certain!)
His power over nature gives hope and comfort through the storms of life.
His power over the heart gives hope for every loved one and every "hopeless" situation.

God is good. He is righteous. He is just. He is faithful and kind. He has loved us with an everlasting love. He reigns in power! Will you end your study with this doxology of hope?

*"Blessing and glory and wisdom, thanksgiving and honor **and power and might**,*
Be to our God forever and ever. Amen."
Revelation 7:12

The Future is Bright

*O*ver and over again, the Scriptures point us to the return of Christ as a source of our hope in this world.

*"Looking for the **blessed hope** and glorious appearing of our great God and Savior Jesus Christ"*

Titus 2:13

*"Blessed be the God and Father of our Lord Jesus Christ, who according to His abundant mercy has begotten us again to a **living hope** through the resurrection of Jesus Christ from the dead, to an inheritance...reserved in heaven for you..."*

1 Peter 1:3-4

He is coming! The future is bright! The sorrows and sufferings of this world will not last forever. All things will be made new.   We will live with Him forever. This is our hope!

Today, *"Set your mind on things above, not on things on the earth."* Why? Because when *"Christ who is our life appears, then you also will appear with Him in glory."*!!! Colossians 3:2,4

1. Spend time simply reading and savoring the wonderful descriptions given about what the future holds for every believer.   Don't worry about taking a lot of notes, but do record at least one thought or phrase that stands out to you as you read each passage.

A Picture of My Future…

a. **Isaiah 60:19-22**

b. Isaiah 65:17-19

c. **John 14:2-3**

d. **Revelation 21:1-4**

e. Revelation 21:22-27

f. **Revelation 22:1-5**

2. Is the world you have just read about real to you? It was to Abraham, and it changed the way he lived.

"By faith Abraham obeyed...And he went out...he dwelt...
for he waited for the city which has foundations, whose builder and maker is God."
Hebrews 11:8-10

The reality of the world to come should change the way every believer lives. In fact, this is exactly what Jesus prayed for just before His death.

a. Read Jesus' prayer for His followers in John 17:14-17.

1) What did Jesus *not* ask the Father to do? (17:15)

2) Instead of asking the Father to take His followers out of the world, what does He ask? (17:15, 17)

3) What means did He ask the Father to use in sanctifying them (setting them apart for a special use or purpose)? (17:17)

4) *(Optional)* If someone asked you how the Word sanctifies a believer, how would you answer?

3. As a Christian, keeping the future in mind will change the way you view this life. How?
With thoughts such as:

Life may be difficult, but a place is being prepared for me.

Loss is painful, but I am never without hope.

Illness might end in death, but death is not the end.

Rejection may hurt, but this is not my home.

Riches are uncertain, but they are not my real treasure.

Can you add to this list?

_____ but _____

_____ but _____

While you obediently wait for the future God has prepared, let His Word encourage you and set you apart for the work He has planned for you here. Keep your thinking focused on eternal truths, as Paul did:

a. Read 2 Corinthians 4:8-9 and fill in the blanks under each column below. (The first one is done for you.)

Paul's Circumstance	*In Light of Eternity*
v. 8 *"hard pressed on every side"*	*"yet not crushed"*
v. 9	

b. Read the following words out loud as you bring your study to an end. Underline the statement that is most significant for your life at this moment.

"Therefore we do not lose heart.
Even though our outward man is perishing,
Yet our inward man is being renewed day by day.

For our light affliction,
which is but for a moment,
is working in us a far more exceeding and eternal weight of glory,
while we do not look at the things which are seen,
but at the things which are not seen."

2 Corinthians 4:16-17

c. In light of who God is and what He has promised, will you be like Abraham and Paul and keep pressing on with an eternal perspective? If so, tell God your desires and commitment as you come before His throne of grace.

Thoughts, Meditations and Prayers

Appendices

Appendix A

Dearest Ones,

As the drab winter scene flashed by the car windows I remember thinking, "Kristie has no idea why she asked me to go with her today, but I do." There was no doubt in my mind that the Lord had moved her to invite me to spend the day with her. From the depths of the despair I was feeling, I had to acknowledge that He was keeping me from rashly taking my own life.

I still remember that day and how I felt during that painful time, but I no longer feel the intensity of emotion when I think of those circumstances. It is almost like remembering a story I've read in a book. My life is so different now. The Lord Jesus has brought healing, renewal, and joy to my heart.

How did I get from there to here? God's mercy is great! First of all, He saved me through faith in Jesus Christ and put a new spirit within me. Second, He gave me the Gant family. The whole family ministered to me (even the children, though they did not know it). I am especially grateful for the leadership of Hank Gant in his family, which enabled Kristie to minister to me as she did.

Kristie taught me how to study the Bible. She taught me how to apply Scripture to my life. She rebuked me in my sin. She taught me where to put my hope (in God). She taught me how to pray and what to pray for. She listened…for hours and hours. She literally let me cry on her shoulder. She never told me that I shouldn't feel pain when painful circumstances were the bulk of my experience. She told me she would care and she would hope, even when I didn't care and I didn't hope. She spent hours carefully explaining Scripture and helping me to apply it to my circumstances. In short, God gave me an older woman to teach, train, and love me. How blessed I am!

Third, God showed mercy to me by showing me my responsibilities. I began to study His Word diligently. I repented of the sins He showed me, and I endeavored to put them off. I gave a great deal of time and energy to thinking about the Word and applying it to my circumstances in practical ways. I put on (however imperfectly) the graces of the Christian life and the fruit of the Spirit. I spent much time in fasting and prayer. I took control of my mind, replacing the unbiblical, God-dishonoring thoughts with biblical, God-honoring ones. I listened to wise counsel and did (for the most part) what I was counseled to do. I made mistakes, and there were times of sin and failure where I had to reclaim ground I had already gained, but the overall course of my life became more and more Christ-honoring

There are many reasons you may be doing this study. You may be terribly depressed, you may be trying to learn how to counsel someone who is depressed, or you may simply want to learn how to think biblically.

To those who are depressed, you have my heartfelt sympathy. I know that the circumstances that brought you to this place in your life are painful to *you*. Acknowledge the facts, acknowledge how much it hurts, cry if you need to…but don't stop there! You have a personal responsibility to work, and to work hard: not for an hour, not for a day, but over time…maybe a long time…to reach the point where you can have joy in your salvation and hope in God your Savior.

(Continues on next page)

You may be thinking, "But I have no time, no energy and no one to disciple me." I want you to ask yourself a question. **Consider honestly: "How much time and energy have I put into being depressed and not doing what is right?"** I think you will find that it takes just as much time and energy (maybe even more) to be depressed as it does to obey God. I know that this was true in my case. If the Lord has not given you a wise discipler to teach you face to face, pray and ask Him to bring one into your life. In the meantime, seek out wise counsel in print. Allow yourself to soak up and be taught truth and wisdom from godly authors. (I learned much from writers such as Martha Peace, Elizabeth George, Elisabeth Elliot, and Glenda Revell.)

My particular circumstances were a fairly even mixture of my own sin, others' sins against me, and the difficult providences of God. I could not change the providence of God. I could not change the fact that other people had sinned and were continuing to sin against me.

However, I *could* change my own thoughts, attitudes and actions. I was responsible to deal biblically with my sin through repenting, trusting in Christ, studying the Bible, obeying the Bible, practicing righteousness, praying and fasting. I was responsible to accept God's providence in my life. I was responsible to respond biblically to others' sins against me.

This did not happen overnight.

Slowly but surely I began to change. Crawling gave way to baby steps and stumbles, which gave way to walking, which became running. As I changed, some of my circumstances began to change. Within months, I had the joy of knowing God in a deeper and more intimate way than ever before, as well as the joy of knowing I was being obedient to Him in the midst of terribly difficult circumstances.

As the years have gone by (it will be 10 years as of December 2004), God has restored relationships and answered prayers in ways that I never imagined back in those dark days of despair. Though some of my painful circumstances may never change, at least in my lifetime, and though some new ones have been added, I am different. By God's abundant mercy and grace, I am able to face past, present, and future with hope in God.

All my love,
"Katie"

Those Who
Wait...

Appendix C

Just a Few of God's Promises

"...in Me you may have peace. In the world you will have tribulation; but be of good cheer, I have overcome the world." John 16:33

"...know that the LORD your God, He is God, the faithful God who keeps covenant and mercy for a thousand generations with those who love Him and keep His commandments." Deuteronomy 7:9

"The humble He guides in justice, and the humble He teaches His way." Psalm 25:9

"For the Lord will not cast off forever. Though He causes grief, yet He will show compassion according to the multitude of His mercies." Lamentations 3:31-32

"Through the LORD's mercies we are not consumed, because His compassions fail not. They are new every morning; Great is Your faithfulness." Lamentations 2:22-23

"Fear not, for I am with you; be not dismayed, for I am your God. I will strengthen you, yes, I will uphold you with My righteous right hand." Isaiah 41:10

"And you will seek Me and find Me, when you search for Me with all your heart. I will be found by you, says the LORD..." Jeremiah 29:13-14

"And we know that all things work together for good to those who love God, to those who are the called according to His purpose." Romans 8:28

"Therefore He is also able to save to the uttermost those who come to God through Him, since He always lives to make intercession for them." Hebrews 7:24-25

"For our light affliction, which is but for a moment, is working for us a far more exceeding and eternal weight of glory, while we do not look at the things which are seen, but at the things which are not seen." 2 Corinthians 4:17-18

Promises About His Promises

"...for He who promised is faithful." Hebrews 10:23

"The Lord is not slack concerning His promise..." 2 Peter 3:9

"Blessed be the LORD...There has not failed one word of all His good promise..." 1 Kings 8:56

"God is not a man, that He should lie, Nor a son of man, that He should repent. Has He said, and will He not do? Or has He spoken, and will He not make it good?" Numbers 23:19

"...[God has] given to us exceedingly great and precious promises, that through these you may be partakers of the divine nature..." 2 Peter 1:4

"For as many as are the promises of God, they all find their Yes (answer) in Him (Christ). For this reason we also utter the Amen, (so be it) to God through Him—that is, in His Person and by His agency—to the glory of God." 2 Corinthians 1:20 (Amplified)

"Therefore, having these promises, beloved, let us cleanse ourselves from all filthiness of the flesh and spirit, perfecting holiness in the fear of God."

2 Corinthians 7:1

Appendix D

To a Christian Gentlewoman [23 April 1628]:

My love in Christ remembered to you. I was indeed sorrowful when I left you, especially since you were in such heaviness after your daughter's death; yet I am sure you know that the weightiest end of the cross of Christ that is laid upon you, lies on your strong Savior. For Isaiah said that in all your afflictions He is afflicted (Is. 63:9). O blessed Savior, who suffers with you! Your soul may be glad, even to walk in the fiery furnace, with the Son of Man, who is also the Son of God. Take courage. When you tire, he will bear both you and your burden (Ps. 55:22). In a little while you shall see the salvation of God.

Your lease on your daughter has run out; and you can no more quarrel against your great Superior for taking what He owns, than a poor tenant can complain when the landowner takes back his own land when the lease is expired. Do you think she is lost, when she is only sleeping in the bosom of the Almighty? If she were with a dear friend, your concern for her would be small, even though you would never see her again. Oh now, is she not with a dear friend, and gone higher, upon a certain hope that you shall see her again in the resurrection? Your daughter was a part of yourself; and, therefore, being as it were cut in half, you will be grieved. But you have to rejoice; though a part of you is on earth, a great part of you is glorified in heaven.

Follow her, but do not envy her; for indeed it is self-love that makes us mourn for them that die in the Lord. Why? Because we cannot mourn for them since they are happy; therefore, we mourn on our own private account. Be careful then, that in showing your affection in mourning for your daughter that you are not, out of self-affection, mourning for yourself.

Consider what the Lord is doing. Your daughter has been plucked out of the fire, and she rests from her labors. Your Lord is testing you by casting you into the fire. Go through all fires to your rest. And now remember, that the eye of God is upon the burning bush, and it is not consumed; and He is gladly content that such a weak woman as you should send Satan away frustrated. Honor God now, and shame the strong roaring lion, when you seem weakest.

Should you faint in the day of adversity? Recall the days of old! The Lord still lives; trust in Him. Faith is exceedingly charitable and believes no evil of God. The Lord has placed in the balance your submission to His will and your affection for your daughter. Which of the two will you choose? Be wise; and as I trust you love Christ better, pass by your daughter, and kiss the Son. Men lop the branches off their trees so they may grow up high and tall. The Lord has lopped your branch off by taking from you many children, so that you would grow upwards, setting your heart above, where Christ is at the right hand of the Father.

Prepare yourself; you are nearer your daughter this day than you were yesterday. Run your race with patience; let God have what belongs to Him. Do not ask Him for the daughter who has been taken from you, the daughter of faith; but ask Him for patience, and in patience possess your soul. Lift up your head; your redemption draws near.

Your affectionate and loving
friend in the Lord Jesus,
Samuel Rutherford[1]

Dear _____,

*I*t is hard to know the words to say that would be of an encouragement to you. This is something that doesn't seem to go away...as much as we may wish it would. I can tell you that I love you. That God will work. That God will make a way. That this will all work for your good and His glory. That heaven is not far away. But you know all that.

*Y*our job is to be a picture of the church. If you step out of that role, and go against your husband, God's purposes will not be served. Can you not find some way to submit to him with a happy heart? The church is not to offer grudging submission to Christ...though we often do...as in this case.

I wish I was there to give you a hug. I know how heavy your heart must be. Don't give up. God has a plan. You don't need to know it yet.

*R*emember Elijah? He had a great victory on the mountain...then quickly ended up in despair. He had a huge pity party. Your husband's attitude with you in August was quite a victory...but don't lose faith now. God is able. Faith is believing what you cannot see. I know you don't see how God will work it out...but He will. Have faith. Trust Him. Pray.

*R*emember Judges? God sent oppressors in order to test Israel. When they cried out, He sent a deliverer. Is this a test? I don't know. But it might be. Do you trust Him? How firm is your faith?

*H*as what you have been studying about being in covenant with God been lost on you? The God of the Universe, the Almighty, is your covenant partner. He will defend you. He will fight for you. He will fulfill all His promises to you. Do you not believe this? You don't, if you end up in despair over the words of one mere man. Remember all you just learned about belief/faith/obedience.

*P*aul had doors shut. He was not always allowed to do or to go where he wanted. He didn't pout over the doors God closed...He went another route...and God's will was accomplished. Yet, all the while, he continued to pray for the desires that were in his heart. And God gave him his desires in God's timing and in God's way.

*T*o the Israelites, it looked as if one man, Pharaoh, was responsible for keeping them in slavery. But it was never so. God was always the One who decided where they lived, how they lived, and when they would be set free. And freedom was not an afterthought...it was planned out before it ever started...and ended not a day late.

*W*hat about Martin Luther? God locked him away and he had no voice to the people...but he did translate God's Word into German during all his time in Wartburg Castle. Did his voice not travel farther and louder than if he had been free to teach and preach with his own voice? You have a zeal for study. Does God want to use this ability He has given you in some way you cannot imagine now? I don't know. Maybe there are those who need some insights that only your loneliness and isolation will bring into focus.

*Y*ou've heard me say this so many times before. Don't live by what you feel, live by what you know.

*L*ove Him with all your mind. He loves you with all His heart!

*K*eep praying; God delights to answer the prayers of His children. And, should God choose to answer "wait" or "no" in this life, you DO HAVE a Bridegroom (our Lord Jesus Christ) that is ALL you desire and more; and you will have eternity to enjoy the marriage and love you have always wanted. Respond to Him. Love Him. Trust Him. Lean on Him. And until He comes for you, make ready your wedding garment...of white linen...of righteousness.

*K*eep your eyes on eternity. Call me if you want to talk.

I love you,
Kristie

Endnotes
and Bibliography

Endnotes

About the Study

1. A teacher/leader/discipler guide is available from At Home Studies. For details, visit **athomestudies.com**.

Foundation Studies

Lesson One *Where is Your God?*
1. Lou Priolo, <u>A Biblical View of Depression</u> Cassette tape recording (Chesterton, IN: SWA, Ltd.). Priolo presents material from Psalm 42 and Ecclesiastes 3 in a format similar to the ones I use here and in Lesson Two. Another good resource containing similar thoughts is D. Martyn Lloyd-Jones, <u>Spiritual Depression</u> (Grand Rapids, MI: Wm. B. Eerdmans Publishing Company, 1965).

Lesson Two *How Long, LORD?*
1. Matthew Henry, <u>A Commentary on the Whole Bible</u> Vol. 4 (Old Tappan, NJ: Fleming H. Revell Co.) 137.
2. Henry, 137.

Lesson Three *The Word of Truth*
1. NAS and Amplified translations appear in <u>The Comparative Study Bible</u> (Grand Rapids, MI: Zondervan, 1984). Phillips translation is from J.B. Phillips, <u>The New Testament in Modern English</u> (New York: Macmillan, 1972).
2. Fanny J. Crosby, "I Am Thine, O Lord" <u>Hymns for the Family of God</u> ed. Fred Bock (Nashville: Paragon Association, Inc., 1976) 455.

Lesson Four *God in Perspective*
1. A. W. Pink, <u>The Sovereignty of God</u> (Carlisle, PA: The Banner of Truth Trust, 1959) 9.

Lesson Five *What Do You Know?*
1. Phillip Keller, <u>A Shepherd Looks at Psalm 23</u> (Grand Rapids, MI: Zondervan Publishing House, 1970) 37-38.

Lesson Six *All is Not Lost!*
1. Benjamin Potter, cited in James W. Bruce III, <u>From Grief to Glory</u> (Wheaton, IL: Crossway Books, 2002) 124.

Lesson Seven *From Here to Eternity*
1. Charles Spurgeon, <u>The Power of Prayer in a Believer's Life</u> (Lynnwood, WA: Emerald Books, 1993) 16-20.
2. Spurgeon, <u>Prayer</u> 28.

Names of God

1. Andrew Jukes, <u>The Names of God</u>. (Grand Rapids, MI: Kregel Publications, 1967) 137-141.
2. Frank E. Gaebelein, ed., <u>The Expositor's Bible Commentary</u> Vol. 6 (Grand Rapids, MI: Zondervan, 1992) 246.
3. Issac Watts, "O God, Our Help in Ages Past" Sims, 286.
4. Lawrence O. Richards, <u>Expository Dictionary of Bible Words</u> (Grand Rapids, MI: Zondervan Publishing House, 1991) 537.
5. Warren W. Wiersbe, <u>Classic Sermons on the Names of God</u> (Grand Rapids, MI: Kregel Publications, 1993) 69.
6. Fanny J. Crosby, "He Hideth My Soul" Sims, 272.
7. John MacArthur, <u>The MacArthur Study Bible</u> (Nashville, TN: Word Publishing, 1997) 880.
8. MacArthur, 297.
9. June Titus, <u>Still Living, Still Learning</u> (Grand Rapids, MI: Kregel Publications, 2000) 162.
10. MacArthur, 1700.
11. MacArthur, 1828.
12. Cleland B. McAfee, "Near to the Heart of God" Sims, 301.

Topics on Hope

1. James Strong, <u>Strong's Exhaustive Concordance of the Bible</u>. (Peabody, MA: Hendrickson Publishers). Strong assigned a number to every word in the original languages of the Bible. Many reference works and internet sites use his numbering system. Two easy-to-use word study books that follow Strong's system are <u>The Complete Word Study Old Testament</u> and <u>The Complete Word Study New Testament</u> (see bibliography). Each of these has the entire Old or New Testament text printed out with a number (Strong's number) written above the English words. To find the original word and its definition, simply turn to that number in the back of the book.
2. Warren Baker, ed., and Spiros Zodhiates, <u>The Complete Word Study Old Testament</u> (Chattanooga, TN: AMG Publishers, 1994) 2361.
3. J. Sidlow Baxter, <u>Explore the Book</u> Vol. 3 (Grand Rapids, MI: Zondervan Publishing House, 1966) 70.

Appendices

1. Samuel Rutherford, cited in James W. Bruce III, <u>From Grief to Glory</u> (Wheaton, IL: Crossway Books, 2002) 92-93.

Bibliography

Baker, Warren, ed. and Spiros Zodhiates. The Complete Word Study Old Testament. Chattanooga, TN: AMG Publishers, 1994.

Baxter, J. Sidlow. Explore the Book. 6 Vols. in 1. Grand Rapids, MI: Zondervan Publishing House, 1966.

Bennett, Arthur. The Valley of Vision. Carlisle, PA: The Banner of Truth Trust, 1975.

Berg, Jim. Changed Into His Image. Greenville, SC: BJU Press, 1999.

Bock, Fred, ed. Hymns for the Family of God. Nashville: Paragon Association, Inc., 1976.

Bruce, James W. III. From Grief to Glory. Wheaton, IL: Crossway Books, 2002.

Busenitz, Nathan. Living a Life of Hope. Uhrichsville, OH: Barbour Publishing, 2003.

The Comparative Study Bible. Grand Rapids, MI: Zondervan, 1984.

DeHaan, Dan. The God You Can Know. Chicago, IL: Moody Press, 1985.

Elliot, Elisabeth. Be Still My Soul. Ann Arbor, MI: Servant Publications, 2003.

Gaebelein, Frank E., ed. The Expositor's Bible Commentary 12 Vols. Grand Rapids, MI: Zondervan, 1992.

Gill, John. A Body of Doctrinal and Practical Divinity 1809. Paris, AR: The Baptist Standard Bearer, 1995.

Henry, Matthew. A Commentary on the Whole Bible 6 Vols. Old Tappan, NJ: Fleming H. Revell Co.

Jukes, Andrew. The Names of God. Grand Rapids, MI: Kregel Publications, 1967.

Keller, Phillip. A Shepherd Looks at Psalm 23. Grand Rapids, MI: Zondervan Publishing House, 1970.

Kruis, John G. Quick Scripture Reference for Counseling. Grand Rapids, MI: Baker Books, 1994.

Lloyd-Jones, D. Martyn. Spiritual Depression. Grand Rapids, MI: Wm. B. Eerdmans Publishing Company, 1965.

MacArthur, John. The MacArthur Study Bible. Nashville, TN: Word Publishing, 1997.

Mack, Wayne A. A Homework Manual for Biblical Living Vol. 1. Phillipsburg, NJ: P & R Publishing, 1979.

Mack, Wayne. The Superiority of Biblical Hope. Cassette tape recording. NANC Tape Library. Chesterton, IN: SWA, Ltd.

Phillips, J.B. The New Testament in Modern English. New York: Macmillan, 1972.

Pink, A. W. The Sovereignty of God. Carlisle, PA: The Banner of Truth Trust, 1959.

Piper, John. The Hidden Smile of God. Wheaton, IL: Crossway Books, 2001.

Priolo, Lou. <u>A Biblical View of Depression</u>. Cassette tape recording. L Priolo Tape Library. Chesterton, IN: SWA, Ltd.

Richards, Lawrence O. <u>Expository Dictionary of Bible Words</u>. Grand Rapids, MI: Zondervan Publishing House, 1991.

Rogers, Timothy. <u>Trouble of Mind and the Disease of Melancholy</u>. Morgan, PA: Soli Deo Gloria Publications, 2002.

Sims, Walter Hines, ed. <u>Baptist Hymnal</u>. Nashville: Convention Press, 1956.

Smith, Jerome H., ed. <u>The New Treasury of Scripture Knowledge</u>. Nashville, TN: Thomas Nelson Publishers, 1992.

Spurgeon, Charles. <u>The Power of Prayer in a Believer's Life</u>. Lynnwood, WA: Emerald Books, 1993.

Spurgeon, Charles. <u>The Treasury of David</u> 3 Vols. Peabody, MA: Hendrickson Publishers.

Stone, Nathan. <u>Names of God</u>. Chicago, IL: Moody Press, 1944.

Strong, James. <u>Strong's Exhaustive Concordance of the Bible</u>. Peabody, MA: Hendrickson Publishers.

Tenney, Merrill C., ed. <u>Pictorial Encyclopedia of the Bible</u> 5 Vols. Grand Rapids, MI: Zondervan Publishing House, 1976.

Titus, June. <u>Still Living, Still Learning</u>. Grand Rapids, MI: Kregel Publications, 2000.

Welch, Edward T. <u>Depression: The Way Up When You Are Down</u>. Phillipsburg, NJ: P & R Publishing, 2000.

Wiersbe, Warren W. <u>Classic Sermons on the Names of God</u>. Grand Rapids, MI: Kregel Publications, 1993.

Zodhiates, Spiros, ed. <u>The Complete Word Study New Testament</u>. Chattanooga, TN: AMG Publishers, 1991.

About the Author

Kristie Gant began writing inductive Bible study courses in 2004, after teaching and developing Bible study lessons for over fifteen years. The focus of each of her studies is to teach truth, exalt God, call women to greater obedience, and equip them to disciple their children and other women.

As a child of committed Christian parents, Kristie was taught the Scriptures and at an early age was "made wise unto salvation." (2 Timothy 3:15) Over the years, she has pursued the knowledge of God through inductive Bible study and the reading and hearing of faithful teachers and preachers. The writings of the Puritans have been particularly influential in her understanding of spiritual truths and in her passion for discipleship.

Kristie's Bible study courses have been self-published through *At Home Studies*, a ministry her family began for that purpose. *Hope in God* is her first book to be published on a wider basis. Her other studies include:

- *At Home in the Book of Proverbs: Living Daily in the Wisdom of God*
- *Prayer: Coming to the Throne with Purpose, Passion and Praise*
- *At Home in Book Three of the Psalms: Living Daily in the Presence of God*
- *The Beauty of Holiness: Embracing the Character and Call of God*
- *Thinking Heavenward: Living Daily in Light of Our Eternal Home*

Along with three teacher/leader guides, these courses are currently available through the *At Home Studies* website, www.athomestudies.com.

While attending Texas Tech University, where she received a BA in Speech Pathology, Kristie met and married Hank Gant. They are the parents of two grown children, Amy and Craig. In their local church body, Kristie serves as a women's Bible study leader and teacher. It is the passion of her heart to share the Scriptures with women who love God and who desire that His Spirit progressively transform them into the image of Christ.

My lips shall utter praise,
For You teach me Your statutes.

My tongue shall speak of Your word,
For all Your commandments are righteousness.

Let Your hand become my help,
For I have chosen Your precepts.

I long for Your salvation, O LORD,
And Your law is my delight.

Psalm 119:171-174